Fly-Fishing the Montana Spring Creeks --
The Rainbows of Paradise

John Mingo

Photography: Suzanne Mingo
Fly-tying: Lee Kinsey
Artwork: Mark Susinno
Foreword by Robert Berls

Copyright © 2009 by John Mingo

ISBN 0-7414-5709-1

Cover art from an original oil painting by Mark A. Susinno © 2008.

Published by:

PUBLISHING.COM

1094 New DeHaven Street, Suite 100

West Conshohocken, PA 19428-2713

Info@buybooksontheweb.com

www.buybooksontheweb.com

Toll-free (877) BUY-BOOK

Local Phone (610) 941-9999

Fax (610) 941-9959

Printed in the United States of America

Published December 2009

This book is dedicated to Al Troth, the great American fly tyer, guide, and photographer. Without his insights into fly construction and the fishing of small flies on light, long tippets, we would not have been able to achieve these modest advances in fishing to difficult fish in clear waters.

Contents

Foreword

John Mingo, a "nymph guy" to his friends, asserts that taking trout on nymphs "is more pleasurable than on a dry fly" and that "nymphing is a more complex art than dry fly fishing." John is well aware that such views are not the prevailing opinion in trout fishing, especially trout fishing on those North American equivalents of the English chalk streams, the spring creeks. John asks why is so much fuss made over the dry fly, and why the dry fly purist is considered a cut or more above the nymph fisherman? Even now, as John observes, the legacy of Frederic Halford is still alive.

To answer those questions, even in the short format of a Foreword, requires a journey into history. Tony Hayter, the English scholar of fly fishing, and biographer of Halford, notes that when G.E.M. Skues published his *Minor Tactics of the Chalk Stream and Kindred Studies* in London in 1910, his first, tentative, book-length exposition into fishing the up-stream wet fly, the book "although written in measured and polite prose, was in fact a bombshell." *Minor Tactics*, Hayter asserted, sent "seismic shocks through the fly fishing world for decades to come." "Even today,' Hayter concludes, 'the shrapnel is still flying." The book was a direct threat to Frederic Halford and the cult of the dry fly.

Field sports in early nineteenth-century England were very different than they were to become by the early twentieth-century. The trout fishing of the early nineteenth-century can only be described as loose. At the famous and prestigious Houghton Fishing Club on the River Test, England's premier chalk stream (the Houghton is England's oldest fishing club, founded 1822) members pleased themselves how they wanted to fish. They fished the light, wind-driven, blow line with live Mayflies or grannom sedges. Members bait-fished for trout and perch. If fishing had not been good and members wanted fish to send home, a drag net could be resorted to. Artificial flies were used, mostly in the evening when the wind was down and blowing wasn't possible.

In late-Victorian England all this loose fishing was to change. By the end of the century, England had moved from a mostly localized, provincial, agricultural society where the aristocracy and landed gentry, and particularly the hereditary owners of the great estates, controlled the political system, to a mostly urban, industrial, mass society. In those years of urbanization and industrialization from about 1870 to 1914 the English middle-classes discovered sport. Sport became caught up in a class society anxious to define itself in a very new world. There was a systematic emphasis on amateurism as the criterion of upper-and middle-class sport. Racing had professional jockeys, but also gentleman riders; cricket its gentlemen and its players (i.e. paid professionals) on the same side. They used different entrances and dressing rooms. The Secretaries of the many golf clubs springing up in Britain (only 17 clubs in 1850, but almost 1500 by 1898), and the Secretaries of the growing number of fly fishing clubs, were known as "Honorary Secretaries" lest they be thought as being paid for their work. Field sports flourished because the aura of participation in such sports, associated with the aristocracy and gentry, were as important as their inherent merits. The first year of rod-licensing in England, excluding Scotland, in 1879, about 9,000 licenses were issued; the number rose rapidly to about 69,000 in 1910. Hardy Brothers and several smaller firms produced 800 fly rods a year in the mid-1880s. Ten years later it had grown to 3,500 a year. Game shooting and yachting showed similar proportional increases.

As John Lowerson, the historian of sport in Victorian and Edwardian England put it: "Late Victorian trout fishing offered its own peculiar variant of the search for ethical purity in sport." That variant was the dry fly. Frederic Halford's first and most influential books *Floating Flies and How to Dress Them* and *Dry Fly Fishing in Theory and Practice* appeared to a receptive audience in 1886 and 1889 respectively. John Waller Hills (a Member of Parliament and a Privy Councillor to the Crown) in his 1936 memoir, *My Sporting Life*, wrote that Halford's first book was "a revolution and a revelation." Skues described Halford's second book as "stunning, hypnotic, submerging." Halford had given the dry fly its myth. Halford's 1889 book was a "manifesto of a movement," because Halford was writing about what he believed to be a revolutionary technique which he intended and expected to establish "a dry fly code of practice which would replace all other methods of fishing on the chalk streams." Skues observed that "The dry fly on chalk streams became at first a rage and then a religion." Why did the dry fly transpose from a rage to a religion with moral force?

John Waller Hills, in his sporting memoir, asserted that "That anyone should dare to attack (chalk stream trout) with anything that sank was regarded as indecent. It was hardly the pursuit of a gentleman." That was the crux of the matter: the urge to gentrification. The English writer and biographer, A.N. Wilson, observed that "the urge to gentrify itself...is endemic in the British middle class." The urge to gentrification was one of the great themes and struggles of Victorian Britain. George Kitson Clark, in his classic book, *The Making of Victorian England*, asserted that "the existence of (social) aspirations, and the uncertainty of social definition, led...to an agonizing problem which possibly in the nineteenth century caused more trouble and heart burning in well-nourished bosoms than any other secular problem: who were gentlefolk and who were not?" The historian of the British aristocracy, David Cannadine, shows that the "Victorians were obsessed with" class. Cannadine delineates how "the changes in social identity wrought by the industrial revolution in Britain were imposed on to an elaborate and pre-existing hierarchy of ranks and orders" where the upper-class of aristocracy and gentry still largely controlled the government and were the social leaders. Benjamin Disraeli saw that for many businessmen "concern about status was ultimately more decisive than concern about income...." Upper-middle class men (a rapidly growing class just below the aristocracy and gentry) in Victorian England who had newly-made fortunes (such as Frederic Halford who made his fortune by age 45 and never worked again) yearned for the social status to match their wealth. Such men were eager to be seen as gentlemen. If one had wealth, but not the clear indicators of gentlemanly status (presence in or descent from the aristocracy or gentry; attendance at one of the ancient public schools such as Eton or Winchester; or one of the ancient universities) the only way to be sure you were a gentleman was to be treated like one. Fishing anything but the dry fly could not be risked by such men.

Jack Hills chronicled the shift in practice on many waters to where a dry-fly-only rule was enforced. By 1900 the wet fly had largely disappeared from the chalk streams. Whether there were rules banning it or not, the "cult of the dry fly," as Halford himself called it, had won out. Even the mighty Houghton Club on the Test was to be pressured by the dry fly cult. William Lunn, the highly regarded river keeper at the club (Jack Hills wrote a book about him) from 1887 to 1932, devised several sunk patterns for the chalk streams, but Lunn had to keep quiet about them.

Skues recovered the old wet-fly art and transformed it for modern conditions of sport on the chalk streams. Skues knew that chalk-stream trout fed on nymphs for hours and days at a time letting the hatched-out insect go by. Most chalk-stream anglers were unaware of this, and kept casting dry flies at trout which were seen to be breaking the surface. Halford knew these to be bulging rises and advised the dry-fly men to cast only to trout seen to be taking the hatched-out, upright-winged dun.

Skues' observations of the overwhelming propensity of chalk-stream trout to feed on nymphs were confirmed by his analyses of stomach contents. "Up to the present,' he wrote in a 1930 article, 'I do not think there has been a trout whose stomach has yielded two-percent of winged duns. Nymphs, nymphs, nymphs, all nymphs." In the fourth, 1949, edition of *The Way of a Trout with a Fly*, Skues added a chapter called "The Constant Nymph," referring to the predilection of trout to feed on nymphs over duns: "The strong attraction of the constant nymph." In his posthumously published *Itchen Memories* of 1951, Skues declared that "for several years past, therefore, I have only fished the floating fly when I was definitely convinced that that was what the trout were taking...." In his "Constant Nymph" chapter Skues summed up: "...the angler who offers his trout a proper pattern of nymph stands a better chance of sport than does one who offers it a floating fly. He asserted that the nymph "has the merit of superseding or getting over serious difficulties and limitations of the dry fly...." Skues thought that his nymph fishing was a new art, or perhaps he thought it was "fairer to say, a new phase of an old and largely forgotten art." Jack Hills was right that Skues led a counter-reformation of the wet fly against the dry fly.

The dry fly versus wet fly debate that went on in England from the Victorian and Edwardian years down to and beyond World War II (and continues, attenuated, today) is an instance of the English writer A.N. Wilson's observation that "no quarrel in England is ever about what it seems to be about." Skues' revival of the wet fly on the chalk streams was a direct threat to Halford and the gentleman's dry fly code that Halford had done so much to establish. That is the essence of the debate. On the surface it was a quarrel about two fishing methods, but underneath it was a challenge to the recently established "gentleman's way of fishing" -- the "legitimate method" as Halford liked to call it was now unwritten law.

Skues counter-reformation remained a threat and the dry-fly men brought him to trial. The Flyfishers' Club sponsored a debate on the efficacy and appropriateness of fishing the nymph on chalk streams that was held at the Club on February 10th, 1938. As Skues' biographer, Donald Overfield put it: "You could almost hear the 'Star Chamber' being set up." [The Court of Star Chamber was a medieval, Tudor and Stuart royal trial-court that became a synonym for oppression.] Tony Hayter called the debate "a treason trial." Skues made a concise statement on nymph fishing's effectiveness and appropriateness on the chalk streams and outlined where Halford had gone wrong. The 80-year old Skues was, in effect, prosecuted by the barrister, Sir Joseph Ball. Several other members contributed briefs against the wet fly. Only two members spoke for the defense: Dr. Walshe and Jack Hills. Dr. Walshe put the issue precisely: "Nymph fishing is either no good because it won't catch fish, or no good because it catches too many and destroys the fishery. When these sophistries fail…they play their trump card and call nymph fishing bad form and unsporting. Your modern dry-fly purist who is an ecclesiastic manqué threatens the incorrigible nymph fisherman with the ban of being no sportsman. …Nothing so paralyzes…as the suspicion that we are no sportsman when we go a-nymphing. The choice before us then is to be prigs or no-gentlemen. I hope you will agree to join me in being no gentlemen and continue to nymph." Opinion at the debate went heavily against Skues. If the club members had been sitting as a jury, they would have found Skues guilty of fomenting public disorder.

Vestiges of the "gentlemanly ideal" of the dry fly remain. Several years ago I was fishing the upper Test in the Mayfly (green drake) hatch. While my gillie was occupied with reviving and releasing a trout I had just caught, I saw a nice fish rise downstream and began to drift a fly down to it. The gillie stopped me in mid-drift: "We don't do that here', he said, 'it's too killing a technique if you know what you're doing and you look like you do." That I would have released the trout, as the gillie knew, made no difference. "Too killing a technique" was just a conscious or unconscious excuse: one does not cast downstream in the gentlemanly ideal.

Halford's "legitimate method" is still with us, where a simple fishing technique was made into a moral imperative because of the social insecurities and social strivings of a generation. Let us exorcise the "cult of the dry fly" and fish both the nymph and the floating fly without regard to spurious moral issues. John Mingo's book shows us how.

Robert H. Berls
September 2009
Washington, D.C.

Preface

On a recent mid-July day, Suzanne and I headed to Armstrong Spring Creek. Because it was a Saturday and because the Yellowstone River was still in run-off we knew that at least 12 fishermen would be plying the creek's fertile waters. So we bypassed the main parking lot and went on to the upper water, above the main spring, where the creek is shallow, like an Eastern limestone stream. The fish here are spooky, the clear shallow water betraying the angler unless he casts from the bank and usually downstream with a slack-line cast.

Suzanne headed downstream from the car, to where the upper creek meets the main spring. In those waters she was soon into a pile of fish, before some anglers from below came up to look longingly at her success. I fished the upper water, where the water gets narrower and narrower as I moved upstream. I hooked my fair share of fish, mostly brownies, using a variety of tools that you will read about if you make it through this book. After a few hours, we had a quick lunch and headed back down to the main parking lot.

The big pool there was now relatively absent of anglers, and I waded in between fishermen at the extreme ends of the pool. For the next two hours I used variations of the Slightly Sunken nymph technique to hook 11 nice fish, while my two partners together hooked less than half that amount. I was not in competition with these anglers. I give you the numbers to demonstrate that being able to use a variety of very refined techniques is critical to your success as a spring creek angler. In particular, on this day, as on many others, the fish were feeding fairly steadily on a succession of freshly hatched duns (PMDs hatching uncharacteristically late in the day), on floating nymphs, on nymphs a few inches under the surface, and on midge pupae that hang in the surface or rise toward the surface.

Amidst this activity, my focus was on the fact that essentially no fish were truly rising, and rising steadily, to surface imitations. No dry fly, nor any floating nymph, would have done well in this situation. Every once in a while a new fish made a splashy, real surface rise, but then that same fish would fail to surface for many more minutes. I did not waste valuable fishing time by using my surface imitations. Rather, I concentrated on another set of facts -- that I could see many of the feeding fish holding beneath the surface, that these fish were actively nymphing (or taking pupae) and that each individual fish conducted the bulk of its feeding at a different depth than other fish. Some of the trout were suspended just two or three inches under the surface, others held above the weed beds, but maybe a full foot under the surface, while others held at about mid-depth, over exposed gravelly sections of the pool.

Each fish that I caught during the two hours was engaged with no more than two or three casts before I changed terminal gear or switched to another target. Every single one of the fish that I hooked was a "sighted fish" in which I struck to the movement of the fish. Yet, I was using what is commonly known as a "strike indicator." But I did not watch this indicator -- it was performing two other roles besides telling me when to strike. It carried the nymph or pupa imitation at exactly the right depth for the particular trout to which I was casting. It also told me exactly where my fly was at all times relative to the trout. When I saw the trout turn toward the indicator I set the hook -- well before the indicator had a chance to do its indicating. If I were to wait, the trout would reject the hook before the indicator moved, even though the indicator may have been placed only 6 inches up from the fly!

My choice of flies on that day was not terribly important. In those 2 hours, during which I covered no more than 40 feet (linearly) of pool, I used only two types of size 18 pheasant tail nymphs (one un-weighted on a fine wire dry fly hook, the other weighted under its thorax on a heavier hook). I also took a few fish on an un-weighted, very ordinary black midge pupa imitation. But while my flies were not atypical, everything else that I did was very, very different from what you have read about in books on spring creek fishing. As you read what I write below, you must have an open mind in order to gain from these pages. During those 2 hours on the big pool on Armstrong's, here is what my tackle looked like and what I was trying to accomplish with my casting.

- I was using an 8.5 foot 3-weight rod loaded with a 2-weight WF floating line.

- My leader was over 15 feet long, with the tippet itself comprising 5 feet of this length.

- The tippet was rated at 8x although it was closer to a true 0.004" in diameter. This fine, long tippet will land any fish in front of me because of the built-in stretch of the tippet, the light fly-line and my experience in quickly landing fish with such light tippets. I would not dream of using 8x tippets with the tippet lengths commonly used in most leader constructions (tippets of 24" to 30" in length); they break far too easily.

- In order to turn over this extremely long tippet I cannot use ordinary casting techniques based on slow casting rhythms that look so good on film.

- The tippet is thin because it more important to keep tippet size small when fishing under the surface than when fishing on the surface, since the surface obscures things and makes tippet size less important. Nymphing requires smaller tippet diameters than dry fly fishing, both because of the clarity under the surface and because of the need to allow the micro-currents to make the fly bob and weave as it moves downstream to the trout's mouth.

- When I made my casts to each trout that day, I counted on having a very short drag-free float of perhaps 2-feet in length. I never mend line -- doing so only serves to educate that trout or another as to the artificiality of my offering. I pick up my cast as soon as it is past the specific trout to which I am fishing. I don't hope to achieve a 4-foot drag free float.

- My "strike indicator" looks like nothing you've probably ever used. It is cut with a pair of fly-tying scissors to be smaller than the wing case on the size 18 nymph I am using, often much smaller. My cast must be to the exact spot I am looking at, for if my cast is off by a foot or two, I will never be able to see the indicator and use it to help me keep track of the fly in relation to the fish.

- When my cast hits the water, and once I've caught sight of the indicator, I stop watching it. I watch instead the trout and try to pick up an indication of the trout taking the fly.

- When the trout gives me its indication, my setting of the hook looks to the untrained eye as nothing short of violent -- it is very quick but very short. And I never strike by raising the fly rod upward into the air, always it is moved in parallel to the surface of the water. But the violent strike does not endanger the 8x tippet, and when the hooked trout makes its first strong run downstream, I do nothing but wait for it to stop and hope that it has not buried itself in the weeds or gone under a log. Then, I play it all the way back upstream to my net or, if it is an especially nice fish, I wade down to it. My percentage of lost fish is about the same as that of an experienced angler using 6x tippet. Most of my lost fish are lost by the hook tearing through its flesh and returning to me. Usually this is a result of my striking too late, when the fish has already opened its mouth to reject the fly, and the hook then catches in the very edge of the mouth, in loose flesh.

- Finally, and most importantly, while I was using that day only a couple types of fly (a pheasant tail and a midge pupa), I carefully adjusted the density of the fly (whether it has any weight in it, for example), and the distance from the indicator to the fly, on each individual fish I attacked. I noted carefully how far under the surface the fish was feeding, and I made these adjustments continuously after only one or two casts to a particular fish. And when I made these adjustments, I often made them after I had turned my attention to another target, before I returned again to the fish that initially refused my offering. This constant switching of tactics requires experience and the use of something other than the old-fashioned "greasing" of the tippet to suspend the fly or the new-fashioned use of large bobber-like indicators that scare the fish or, worse, cannot be easily adjusted as to their distance from the fly.

This summary description of my technique, if it hasn't already turned you off as "too technical", is what this book is about. Be patient and plow through these pages and you will be rewarded. Here, I record what I've learned in almost 40 years of fishing these difficult waters. You will find a lot that's new to you and a lot that is over a century old.

Enjoy.

1. Introduction.

The Montana of my youth, in 1969, was a very different place than now. I was a brand-new, lowly Assistant Professor of Economics at the University of Montana, eager to teach inquiring young minds the symmetry of economics, and learn, for myself, the beauty of fly-fishing. What better place to pursue these goals, I thought, than Missoula, Montana. Within a half-hour drive of my tiny office were the Clark's Fork of the Columbia, the Bitterroot, the Blackfoot of Norman Maclean's "A River Runs Through It," and, within 45 minutes, the very-blue-ribbon Rock Creek. I was already an accomplished fisherman, or so I thought, when I arrived that year in Missoula, with all our earthly belongings in a small U-Haul truck, a very pregnant wife at my side. What better place, I thought, to make my transformation complete, to become a real fly-fisherman, skilled and knowledgeable, a catcher of many trout.

The setup was perfect. New professors teach about 9-12 hours a week, prepare for classes and meet with students for about another 18 hours a week, and spend the rest of the time hunting and fishing. For $10,500 a year in salary and benefits this deal was all one-sided. Every afternoon during the school months, I could find time to slip away to one of my home rivers. In the fall, pheasant and duck hunting interfered with my progress as a fisherman, but I endured. My colleagues were all fly fishermen, of course, and there was no lack of effective instruction. It also helped that the Chairman of the economics department was my chief mentor and saw to it that my classes were always in the morning, never when the evening spinner flights appeared on the Clark's Fork. Bob Wallace taught me about the Salmon-fly hatch on Rock Creek and how to make the most of opening day on Buffalo Ford on the Yellowstone. Bob and I were out pheasant hunting when Suzanne went into labor. We rushed back to Missoula with our six birds just in time for me to catch the delivery of our first-born. I took a tongue-lashing for that one, but I couldn't help thinking: "Six birds and a new son -- I'll never be able to top this one."

Life was idyllic, alright. Moreover, the trout of my home rivers were almost always cooperative. Within a couple of years I had developed a pretty good routine of car fishing. This was pretty much just like truck hunting. We would drive down the frontage road along the Clark's Fork west of town and watch for pods of rising rainbows. It was unusual to see more than one or two other fishermen in over twenty miles of river, and we could pretty much pick which pod was the widest and longest. Dry flies were the order of the day; in fact, I simply never learned to fish a streamer or a nymph. It was just a matter of driving or walking far enough to get over a riser, or thirty. The Clark's Fork west of Missoula is a big river, often deep, and always wide. So there were any number of times when I shipped water while wading, and one instance when I had to swim for my life. But fooling the trout was never an issue, only whether my cast could cover them.

Swisher and Richards' book, <u>Selective Trout</u>, had not yet been published in 1969, and even if it had, I did not yet know that the literature on fly-fishing should be an essential part of my education. And, of course, the concept of "selectivity" held no meaning in an environment where no other fishermen competed for my trout and where a "smart" trout could be avoided simply by walking down to the next, always dumber, fish. Tippets in those days were measured in pounds-test, not "Xs." Generally, I could get away with 6 pound test, which, given the technology of the time, meant I was fishing with 2x or 3x tippets most of the time. The flies were almost always Wulff variants or other high-floating creatures. If I really, really wanted to take a tough fish, I would occasionally resort to a size 18 Royal Wulff. It did not matter whether the particular fly imitation was that of a mayfly or caddis, because I, after all, did not <u>know</u> that there was a difference between these orders of insect. A stonefly was big and dark; if the fish were eating something else, then it must be small (size 14, for example) and not so dark. That's all I knew and all I needed to know.

Well, not really. There was still the matter of presentation and, as the Missoula years unwound, I learned that casting by laying the fly line upstream of the leader and tippet often meant the difference between a take and a refusal. I did not know that this type of cast was called the "reach cast," for that term too had not yet been invented. But presentation, of a dry fly, never a nymph, was essentially all that mattered, and I never carried with me more than a half-dozen types of dry flies, varying only in size, in case I ventured upon one of those sippers that seemed so wimpy and fussy. It never occurred to me to wonder why I could not catch some of those fish. My score at the end of the day was always pretty high, and I, although poor, was as happy as any fisherman since old Isaac.

Then came the event that transformed my life (no, this is not hyperbole, I mean it). It was not an epiphany -- more like a slow dawning. It began with one of my colleagues, Bob Vernon, telling me about a stream he had read about in one of those river catalogues -- you know what I'm talking about, a book that lists all the trout streams of Montana, or all the trout streams West of the Divide, or some-such thing. Armstrong Spring Creek was supposed to be the "best damn fishing in the state, if not the country." This could not possibly be more than publisher's hype, I thought. How could this little stream possibly be better than my Clark's Fork? But Bob persisted, and in the summer of 1971 we took the long drive over to Livingston early one morning, intending to fish the day, sleep over in the car, fish the next morning, and return to Missoula that night.

We arrived at the creek around 10 in the morning, just in time for a hatch that I know now as the Pale Morning Dun.[1] This was the first Bob or I had ever seen the West face of the Absarokas – this side looks entirely different than when you drive along I-90 from Billings toward Missoula. In Paradise Valley, eight miles south of the Interstate, the mountains present a much more rugged, forbidding view. In late June there is usually still snow above tree-line, the grasses of Paradise valley are bright green, as are the trees and bushes along the spring creeks. As you drive along the O'Hair ranch road toward the parking lot at Armstrong's, this view -- of the creek, the hayfields, glimpses of the Yellowstone beyond, and beyond that the Absaroka range itself -- never fails to excite. I can remember that day, almost 40 years ago as clearly as my most recent trip to the creek.

Then, there was no fee fishing. Trout Unlimited had arranged with the O'Hair family to allow 10 fishermen, or 10 "rods," per day to fish the creek. TU had put up ten wooden "fish" on the fence posts at the parking lot. One side of each fish was painted red, one side green. When you arrived in the parking lot, you were to turn over a green fish to make it red. When all 10 fish were red, the creek was full, and additional fishermen were supposed to continue on down the valley. As we pulled into the lot, there were four remaining green fish, and I remember thinking to myself that we ought to count the actual number of fishermen to see whether this wooden fish routine was really working.

---

[1] The PMD of the Paradise spring creeks has undergone some substantial taxonomic changes over the decades. For a while, it was considered to be *ephemerella infrequens*, then *lacustris*, now *inermis*. For the reader interested in such things, Purdue University maintains a wonderful website on Mayflies of North America – "Mayflies Central" (go to www.entm.purdue.edu/Entomology/research/mayfly/mayfly.html).

I never got to count the fishermen. Before we strung our rods, we walked to the creek, and that sight is still with me today. Fish were rising everywhere. In front of us, in the parking lot riffle, with no fisherman in sight, there were at least two dozen risers that I could count. We both contracted a good case of buck fever. Rods were hastily assembled. Leaders and tippets were tied on, screwed up, broken off, and re-tied. Finally, I entered the riffle, minus my net, which I had forgotten in the confusion. As it turned out, I didn't need the net, not that morning, not that afternoon, not until evening when a smallish rainbow took pity on me and impaled itself on my size 20 Royal Wulff. Despite a steady procession of insects and rising fish, continuing off and on throughout the day, that was it -- one smallish rainbow. We decided not to stay over. We had been thoroughly whipped, and during the drive back to Missoula, there were no words spoken of such significance that I can recall them today. Bob got over the incident fairly quickly. From that day forward he led a normal life, I am told, though we have lost touch. But that day on Armstrong's began for me what has become a life-long obsession with spring creeks in general, and with the spring creeks of Paradise Valley in particular.

2. Dogma.

The spring creeks of Montana's Paradise Valley are justifiably famous for their prolific hatches and free-rising trout. Every year, articles about the creeks and their hatches appear in *Fly Fisherman* and other angling journals. And some good books in recent years have featured the creeks, including two especially good ones, Darrel Martin's *Micropatterns* and John Shewey's *Mastering the Spring Creeks*. Armstrong's, Nelson's, and DePuy's are famous not because of the scenery (which is spectacular), or because there are so many fish (about 3000 to 7000 per mile depending on who is doing the estimating, in streams that average less than 50 feet wide), or because the hatches are so predictable. They are famous because the fishing can be so damn frustrating -- dozens of rising fish will be within easy casting distance, but the angler will have a hard time connecting. While even beginners can catch a few trout per day on the creeks (there always being at least some dumb fish in such a large population), there are very few anglers that consistently score throughout the day. During the peak of the hatches, most fishermen will experience some great fishing on the surface. But during the rest of the day, when the rises are sparse, hours will go by without most folks hooking-up.

As in any type of fly fishing, the old saying applies: "10% of the fishermen catch 90% of the fish." But, why? And how can you become one of those lucky few? The answers will not necessarily be found in this book. If your skills and experience are average, you certainly will *not* be able to read this book then go out and find success at 8 hookups per hour throughout the day. But, if this book does its job, it will help you understand the *process* of learning to become a good spring-creek fisherman, especially a good spring creek *nymph* fisherman. In a sense, this book is not about spring creeks *per se*, not even the Paradise Valley creeks. It is about a philosophy for fishing over selective fish on rich waters with competition from other knowledgeable anglers. It is about how to *prepare* for a day's outing on tough waters -- planning an "attack" and executing the "game plan." It is about keeping an open mind, rejecting dogma and being receptive to change.

My own game plan for the spring creeks has changed considerably over the more than 35 years I have fished them. By the late 1970s, the creeks had become world-famous, yet nymphing during the 1970s and much of the 1980s was easy. One day, I was standing in a favorite riffle, my rod in the crook of my arm, talking to a local real estate developer about land values. My fly -- a size 16 pheasant tail -- came loose from the hook keeper and fell into the stream below me. In a flash, a 16" rainbow took the fly as it was swinging back and forth in the current. But those good old days are gone. With fame has come increased competition. Not only do experienced anglers now pay up to $100 per day to fish the creeks, but they come armed with the latest in fly patterns and techniques. The many spring creek guides (including the several really good ones like Lee Kinsey – more on him later) constantly must change their tactics to have any hope of getting their clients hooked up with fish. My own techniques have had to change too over the years, and these refinements I will share with you. The reader's goal should be nothing less than becoming a skilled practitioner in the art of fishing small flies on light tippets over tough fish. These skills, once learned and honed, can be used anywhere there are trout to be found in water that allows the use of floating fly lines -- in other words, in almost all waters that hold trout.

To begin, it might be useful to rid ourselves of some traditional thinking on spring creek fishing. Dogma exists in any discipline, but fly fishing seems to have more than its fair share. And spring creek fishing seems to attract dogmatic thinking more than almost any other fly fishing sub-discipline (with the possible exception of Atlantic salmon fishing). Here is a list of "commandments" that one hears or reads a lot. Look at this list. As you progress through the book, you will find each concept challenged, even turned on its head.

1) Dry flies should be fished upstream; wet flies should be fished across and down.

2) Dry fly fishing requires lighter tippets than nymph fishing.

3) Strike indicators should be used when nymph fishing and when the fly-fisher is relatively unskilled. [Sub-commandments: Strike indicators are used to detect a strike. Strike indicators are not needed for dry fly fishing.]

4) Dry fly floatant should be used on the fly to make it float; fly "sink" should be used on the leader to make it sink.

5) When nymph fishing, incorporate weight into the construction of the fly when possible (rather than pinching lead onto the tippet).

6) Nymphs are best used in faster water such as riffle areas, while dry flies are most effective on flat water.

7) Brown trout are smarter than rainbows.

8) Fish are tougher to catch during hatches of very small flies, such as midges.

9) During the *Baetis* hatches, the fishing is better on cloudy days.

10) The fly reel is the least important piece of equipment.

I'm sure the experienced reader can craft some more commandments of his or her own, but I thought exactly 10 would be a nice touch. Some of you, after reading this list, already have thought up situations in which the reverse would be true for a particular commandment. Others, though, might be scratching your heads over some of these. Let's take number 7 -- brown trout are smarter than rainbows. Everybody has heard the expression "wise old brownie," especially in the context of "he didn't get that old or that big by being stupid." But brown trout are not smarter than rainbows, they are actually dumber. Yes, it is true that, as a generalization, browns are often harder to catch than rainbows. This is because brownies generally are more shy than rainbows. In the spring creeks, browns often take up the most difficult lies, at the margins of the streams. Often these lies require the skills of a good caster. But the rainbows are far more selective than the browns, in the sense that if a good float is achieved over the brownie he will be less likely to refuse the fly than will the rainbow.

The rainbows of Paradise are smart -- but they are not shy. Indeed, they are often quite aware of your presence and seem downright arrogant in their view of your incompetence. In the days before Armstrong's and DePuy's had solely wild trout (yes, there were hatchery operations on the streams), the rainbows could be seen occupying the lies in the main part of the stream, while the browns were found on the margins. A sporadically feeding fish, next to some weed bed, was likely to be a brownie, while the fish steadily sipping away in the dead center of the stream was almost always a rainbow. This all changed during the floods of 1996 and 1997. Today, the brownies are so numerous that many small browns can be found in the center of the stream.

Unlike the brownie, the rainbow protects itself *primarily* by being selective. Even if the float is a good one, the rainbow will drift back with the fly, inspecting its construction. Refusals, however, can be counteracted by switching patterns or sizes. For the brownie, a refusal is often simply because the fly dragged. The brownie knows it is not real because of its action, not because of its appearance. Furthermore, the brownies often are less tolerant of the fisherman. Rainbows generally will let you approach to a much closer position (thereby making it easier to achieve a drag-free float). They know you are there and they don't care. They can tell when you are trying to deceive them and, at times, it seems they laugh at you.

My friend Joe McMullen used to raise both rainbows and browns in his hatchery on Spruce Creek in Pennsylvania. He says he could never get the browns to use the automatic feeder. In his view, they were dumber and more shy. What you are about to learn in this book is how to hook those arrogant rainbows, and when you do learn how, you are likely to treat browns with something approaching disdain. When the day comes that you release the 14" brown while muttering 'dumb brownie' under your breath, you will know that you have arrived as a spring creek fisherman.[2]

Having anointed the wild Rainbow as my main tutor, I nevertheless must confess that, to me, brown trout are the most beautiful fish on earth.[3] That is why Mark Susinno's wonderful painting of a large brownie graces the cover of this book. It is why I, like many other fly fishermen, prefer to go after a large brownie more than any other kind of trout. Indeed, the free-rising brownies of the Montana spring creeks, of the Missouri below Holter Dam, and in the Madison's famous riffles, are the main reason we live in this beautiful place.

---

[2] All of the techniques discussed here for the Rainbows of Paradise will work on the other Monatana spring creeks -- except that you will have to practice stealth much more than on the Paradise Valley streams. Casting short distances, as you will learn later, is a key to success, but on these other spring creeks -- Big Spring Creek, Poindexter Slough, the Gallatin Valley creeks -- getting close, without spooking the fish, often means casting from a kneeling position on the bank, not simply wading closer.
[3] And when the brown trout is wild and the rainbow is stocked, as in the English chalk streams, the rainbow is definitely not the smarter of the two.

8

3. Education of a Nymph Fisherman.

The episode on Armstrong's in 1971 was the furthest thing from my mind when the call came to leave our insular world in Missoula and head back to the East -- this time not as a poor Assistant Professor, but as a real live economist with the Federal Reserve Board. The trout of the Clark's Fork could wait for two or three years, I thought, until I had established my reputation in my chosen career. When we were ready to return to Montana, the reasoning went, I would be welcomed back as a Full Professor, with an even lighter teaching load, and more salary with which to buy flies and equipment. I was so sure of success that the week before we packed up and left Missoula I bought a bamboo fly rod (a second-hand Orvis) because, after all, all the East coast fly-fishermen were snobs, and I couldn't be seen on those Eastern streams with my Fenwick fiberglass rod, now, could I?

So, Suzanne and our two young sons and I headed back into the great unknown -- unknown in the sense that we were not really sure what kind of trout fishing could be had within a morning's drive of Washington, D.C. I was born and raised outside of Philadelphia, and the Yellow Breeches was well known to me as a dynamite trout stream for bait fishing, but were there really hatching insects and rising fish? This, I did not know. Nor had I yet discovered the lime-stoners of the Cumberland Valley. But Washington, D.C., it turned out, was chock full of dedicated fly-fishers, and even then, in the fall of 1972, by the end of a single Trout Unlimited meeting, I had met enough folks to feel mildly optimistic about how the two years would go.

One Saturday morning the next spring, I headed out for Chambersburg, PA, to follow the map I had been given of Falling Spring Branch. Falling Spring is a little jewel, I had been told, clear as a bell and full of rising fish. It would, at the least, take my mind off the Montana I was already missing. So, with high hopes I parked the car at Edwards Ave. and strung the Orvis. The pool just upstream of the road already had a few rising fish and it was easy enough to get a cast over them right from the culvert, with no trees to hinder my casting. But 90 minutes later, I had yet to stick one of those trout, and for the first time in a year, the image of that day on Armstrong's came to me. What in hell was going on? I was frantically trying every small dry I owned, including my size 20 sparsely tied Royal Wulff, but nothing came of it.

After a while, I noticed an older gentleman watching me from his position sitting on the running board of a red Ford pickup. The truck was parked in a macadam lot just to the right of the flat above Edwards Ave. He must know the landowner, I thought, for there was a No-Parking sign there. I walked over and struck up a conversation -- it was time to take a break anyway, I was getting nowhere with these fish.

Every fly-fisherman worth his salt can remember those few events in his fishing life when important lessons were learned, when circumstances were right, when the right decisions were reinforced by willing fish (or lack thereof). Datus Proper in his well-received treatise on trout fly design said it best when he titled his book "What the Trout Said." The trout that day on Falling Spring were talking to me, although I was yet to understand the nature of their speech. Like the trout on Armstrong's, the fish were telling me that my fly was wrong. I knew it was not my technique, for I actually put down very few fish that day. Indeed, I was getting fairly good drag-free floats and quite a few fish rose to the fly but refused when they got a good look at it. They were definitely talking to me.

But what those trout said that day was less important than what that old guy said. "Those trout giving you a hard time, are they?" "You bet," I said. "What am I doing wrong?" He answered with another question. "Where are you from?" "Well, I just moved to D.C. from Montana," I said, "and this is the first time I've fished Falling Spring." "I could tell that," he said. "Those Montana fish might eat those large, bushy flies of yours, but not the trout on Falling Spring." Large flies? A size 20? Jesus, I thought, I'm in a heap of trouble.

The conversation went on like that for about 10 minutes. I heard the words *Baetis* something or other, and then the words that spoke to me like no trout ever had, before or since. The old guy said I should buy a book, Selective Trout, by Swisher and Richards. I repeated the words several times in my mind so I wouldn't forget them. "There's a shop in Washington called the Angler's Art, you can get it there," he said. He gave me a couple of flies that actually worked on these fish -- at least I wouldn't get skunked -- although I had trouble getting my 5x tippet through the eye of the fly.

The next Monday I stopped into Barry Serviente's shop and bought the book.[4] And in the years

---

[4] Barry no longer concentrates on book sales and The Angler's Art is now headquartered in Plainfield, PA. He

since, I have bought many others. What I am going to share with you, however, is not in those books, at least not in any cohesive fashion. *Selective Trout* and the others will tell you about the stages of the insects; they will tell you how to tie flies to match those stages; and they will tell you how to fish those flies over selective trout -- but they will not tell you how to *learn* to fish, and they will not tell you how to *learn* to fish the spring creeks. What the books taught me was that I had to consider several stages of the mayfly and the caddis -- the nymph or larval/pupal stages, the dun or sub-imago stages, and the spinner or egg-layer (adult) stages. The books also said that the underwater stages of the insects accounted for 90% of the trout's diet. But what I learned on my own is that practice, repetitious practice, is necessary to become an adequate fly-fisher. And that goes double in order to become an adequate nymph fisher. So I made trip after trip to the Cumberland Valley limestoners -- Falling Spring, Big Spring, and Yellow Breeches (the Letort, I was told, would be too tough for me). I chose these three streams to practice because I knew they held lots of fish. Lots of fish were necessary, I reasoned, because nymph-fishing was done mostly "blind." If the trout weren't there to tell me when I was doing it right I would never get the positive reinforcement I needed. To this day, I still see inexperienced fly-fishers trying to learn their art over almost barren water, or water so crowded that even an experienced fly-fisher would get only a few strikes per day -- hardly the amount of positive reinforcement the beginner needs.

So, during those early D.C. years I became a fisher of nymphs. This was a fortunate thing, since "rises" on the eastern streams are an ephemeral (no pun intended) occurrence. Some days, my comrades and I would see absolutely not a single rise-form. Some of my friends would spend their time blind-fishing a dry fly, hoping the occasional fish would take a break from its search for nymphs in order to rise to the artificial.[5] But this was not generally fruitful, and I learned early on that my days of practice were paying off -- my friends started referring to me as the

---

can be reached at 1-800-848-1020 or by e-mail at bserviente@aol.com.

[5] When insect populations are not heavy in a particular stream, the nymphs may not begin their "breaking loose" from the bottom in significant numbers during any given day. Thus, hatching nymphs at the surface do not occur in sufficient numbers to tempt even a single fish to rise. But there still are sufficient quantities of free-drifting nymphs to cause some fish to key in on the insects. In the parlance of the fishing literature, the trout are "looking down," not "up." When you see this phrase it usually is meant to distinguish between a rising fishing versus a nymphing fish. But susceptibility to an artificial nymph, as we shall see, is greatly influenced by where in the water column you fish your nymph. Sometimes the nymph-devouring fish are "looking up" to intercept their prey, while at other times they are truly "looking down".

"nymph guy" -- a title in which I now take some pride.

But those wonderful days on those Pennsylvania streams did not stop my longing for the Montana rivers I loved. And I began to think more and more about that day on Armstrong's, when the trout were talking to me but I could not hear. So, as I began to like my job in Washington more and more, we also began to take our vacations to Livingston. By the mid-70s I had become familiar with Nelson's as well as Armstrong's. DePuy's was still later to become an object of my affection; I became enamored with it largely due to Bob Auger's influence in the 1980s. Suzanne and I bought a plot of land overlooking the Livingston spring creeks, 8 miles south of town, and in 1978 we built a summer home there. I had convinced the Federal Reserve Board to grant me 8 weeks of leave without pay during the summer, and Suzanne was a school teacher, so we could spend our time seriously studying and enjoying the spring creeks each summer. This book is about what I have learned in more than 1000 days on the Paradise spring creeks over the past almost 40 years, as well as countless days on the Pennsylvania limestone creeks, spring creeks in many of the other U.S. states, and in New Zealand, Argentina, Austria, and England.

4. The Weighted Nymph at Right-Angles.

Why is it that so much fuss is made over the Dry Fly? Why is a dry fly purist considered a snob, a nymph fisherman a somewhat lower form of life (although still above that of a spin fisherman)? Even now, in the first decade of a new century, the legacy of Halford is very much alive. In an issue of *Fly Fisherman*, Nick Lyons, author of the well-received book *Spring Creek*, devoted one of his columns to the joys of surface fishing. Lyons, unlike some of his predecessors, however, tells it like it is -- he simply likes dry fly fishing better, likes seeing the fly, seeing the trout appear, as if a mirage under the fly, sucking it in. To Lyons, it is a visual pleasure, not better, just more pleasurable.

But with all due respects to Halford and Lyons, I must confess that I too am a snob -- except, I am a nymph snob. To me, the taking of a trout on a nymph is more pleasurable than on a dry fly.[6] Moreover, nymphing is a more complex art than dry fly fishing, incorporating all of the skills needed to achieve a drag-free float, but adding the dimension of an unseen take. It's been many years now since those early days in Missoula. Back then, like a lot of beginning fly fishermen, I was a dry fly fisher. This was not by choice, not a matter of being cultured or snobbish. Rather, it was the only way I could consistently catch fish. I had tried nymphing several times, even whole hours at a time. But I rarely got any hookups. With the dry fly, I could see everything -- whether or not I had drag, for example -- and I caught fish. Much of the time, I fished the dry fly blind. Even in Montana, hatches don't take place all day long (although, during some times of the year, the Livingston spring creeks come close). So, during the Missoula years, I pitched the dry fly over every likely looking lie or every place where, during an actual hatch, I had seen a fish rising. And I took more than my fair share of fish. These were not sophisticated spring creek trout, after all. When they saw something juicy floating by, they would interrupt their nymphing to rise through 3 or 4 feet of current to take my offering. But all this changed when we moved back East.

---

[6] Nymph fishing was first written about by G.E.M. Skues, and the master himself felt this way (p. 375, <u>Sidelines, Sidelights, and Reflection</u>, 1932) -- "An enthusiastic dry-fly fisher who was vainly endeavoring to persuade a nymph-feeding Itchen trout to accept his floater said to me the other day, 'I like to see my fly taken on the surface; that is the great attraction of trout fishing for me." I replied, "So do I, but I like even more to divine when my nymph has been taken under water.' 'Ah!' he said, 'that is a subtlety which is beyond me."

After the episode on Falling Spring, I took my reading seriously, and I began to watch what was happening around me. I made a lot of new fishing friends during the 1970s, folks I had sought out at the monthly Trout Unlimited meetings. Many of these people were better fishermen than I. Their casting loops were flatter, they knew a lot more about the hatches on the Pennsylvania trout streams, and they were better fly tyers. But I noticed something almost every time we went out together. On those weekend trips to the Breeches, to Penn's Creek, to Kettle, Pine, Slate Run, and dozens of other "name" trout streams, my friends and I spent long hours each day casting dry flies blind to fish that seemed to be firmly rooted on the bottom, refusing even to acknowledge we were there by occasionally inspecting our offerings. Neither my seasoned friends nor I were getting any hookups except during the brief time each day when the actual hatches occurred or, occasionally, during the late evening spinner falls. If I was going to catch fish in the East at anywhere near the rate I was used to catching them in Montana, I had better learn to fish a nymph, and I had better learn fast.

So, I started leaving my dry flies at home. I recommend this approach to anyone who "would love to learn nymphing." It also helps to take the occasional day off during the middle of the week, especially if you live near overcrowded waters. I would head out to the Breeches on a Wednesday morning with only a box of nymphs I had tied using the instructions in Swisher and Richards, along with a container of split shot and some tippet material. I fished the same water over and over again. I knew this water well by now, having taken fish on its surface during the Sulphur hatches of spring. Since I knew the water well, I knew I was fishing over trout. I did not have to worry whether I was standing in the part of the stream where there were fish -- I knew they were there. If I got no strikes, such information was useful to me, for it told me I had to change my terminal tackle or my tactics, or both. But under no circumstances did I use dry flies. Even when, by late morning, trout would begin rising to the duns I could see floating by me, I did not switch to a dry fly -- because I had none with me.

The first nymphing technique I learned in those days is what is considered standard nymphing practice in the textbooks: weight the nymph (or place a split-shot on the tippet 12 inches or so above the fly), cast up and across, gain control of the line, and watch the end of the floating fly line to see if it moves. Try to achieve a drag-free float, just as when casting a dry fly. Back then, I used a 9 ft leader/tippet combination, most often with a 4x tippet and a size 14 hare's ear or similar nymph, and I made relatively short casts, rarely more than 25 feet in length. I did not yet know about the important relationships between leader/tippet construction, amount of split-shot, and the placement of a strike indicator. In fact, I didn't even know strike indicators existed until the late 1970s. These details, you will see, are vitally important to the success rate of the nympher, especially in difficult, much-fished waters. But for the moment we will ignore them, concentrating instead on the nymphing technique itself rather than on the terminal tackle.

What I learned was that it was crucial to maintain a particular relationship between the leader and the floating fly line. In general, I positioned myself opposite a known or suspected lie. I tried to keep the last three feet or so of the fly line at *right angles* to the current's flow as the cast hits the water. This means that, at the end of the cast, the fly *line* must be flipped upstream of a direct line between the angler and the fly (see Diagram 1). This "reach cast" serves a couple of purposes. Initially, it permits the fly to sink rapidly to the strike zone. Then, as the fly comes downstream, and as the angler retrieves excess fly line, the leader (if it is floating and seen) or the end of the fly line is in a position to "show" the angler a strike (by twitching cross-current, out to where the fly is). This right-angle technique also is a critical tool for indicator-fishing. Again, the reach cast serves to place the tippet past the indicator at a right angle to the fish, so that the indicator shows the fisherman a strike by moving out toward the fish.

It was not until the late 1970s that I learned to categorize this type of nymphing in terms of the angler's *position* relative to the fish. That is, the angler stands at a "right angle" to the strike zone (he stands so that the fish is opposite the fisherman rather than upstream or downstream of his position). In this right-angle-nymphing -- indeed, in all types of nymphing -- each cast is made in deliberate fashion, to a very specific, defined strike zone, an area on the bottom of the stream perhaps three feet long by one foot wide. The cast is made to a spot three, four, or even 10 feet upstream of the strike zone, depending on depth of the strike zone and speed of the current. The key to success is learning how to "sense" when the fly is sinking down to and through this strike zone. This is very much a "timing" game; you must be in the perfect position and state of mind to set the hook during the brief moment when the fly is drifting through this strike zone.

The cast must be made to a spot far enough upstream of the strike zone to allow the split-shot to do its job and take the fly down through the current to the fish, arriving at the fish's nose at the *exact moment* when the fly is opposite the fisherman. In faster currents, or in deeper waters, the cast must be made further upstream of the strike zone, or a heavier split shot must be used, or the floating indicator must be placed higher up from the fly, or all three. This is because, in the faster, deeper current, the fly takes longer to get down to a spot in front of the trout's snout. Wait a minute, you say. "In front of the trout's snout?" What trout? What snout? I thought this was "blind" nymphing to an unseen fish. Ah, right you are. But -- and this is the key to all blind nymphing -- you must make every cast to a specific spot in the manner you would if you actually were to see a fish. Even when "shotgunning" to cover as much water as possible, make each cast *as if* to a specific fish. That is, although you are blind-fishing the water with a sunken nymph, on each cast imagine where the strike zone is, imagine how long it will take your fly to reach that depth, and be prepared to strike, when the fly enters the strike zone.

To see how to envision your cast relative to the strike zone, see Diagram 1, below.

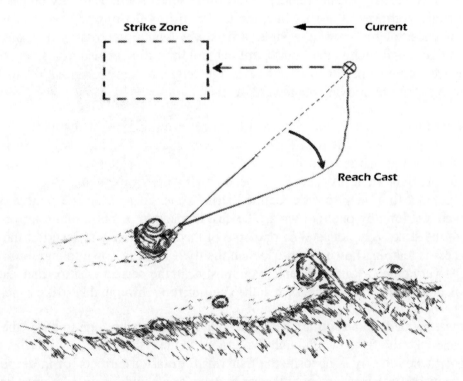

DIAGRAM 1 -- Using a reach cast to place the fly line at a "right angle" to the current.

As the cast hits the water, finish the cast with a reaching motion (or a flip of the last several feet of fly line) to move the fly line so that it lands at right angles to the line of drift of the fly (look at Diagram 2, at position 1, the moment the fly hits the water). Begin to strip in the fly line, taking care not to strip faster than necessary. Keep excess fly line off the water, but allow enough fly line on the water to detect a strike (several feet of fly line at least). We will discuss the use of strike indicators later. For now, you are using the end of the fly line to detect a strike -- but the use of an indicator doesn't change the basic technique of this right-angle nymphing.) Finally, keep the rod tip <u>at waist level or lower</u> (in order to be in a good position to strike when the time comes).

This is not the "high-sticking" method taught in some textbooks (such as the one by Charles Brooks). It is a more delicate form of nymphing in which, during the float, the angler is trying to achieve a presentation that is much the same as when using a dry fly. To achieve a drag-free float at the distances involved, some amount of fly line must remain on the water, unlike the high-sticking technique which calls for only the leader to be in the water at the time when the fly passes the angler.

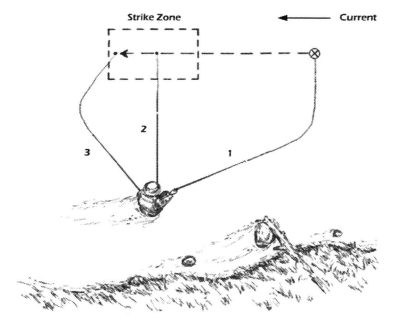

DIAGRAM 2 -- Remain aware of the position of the rod tip as the drift continues.

Be aware at all times of where you keep your rod *tip* as the fly line floats past you. Keep the rod tip low and as near to a right angle with the line of drift of the fly as possible. Think about only two things: *when* is the strike indicator (the end of the fly line, say) going to hesitate or dip forward, and *in which direction* are you going to drive the tip of the rod when the strike comes. The beginning nympher, using this sunken nymph technique, spends his time wondering if he will be able to detect the strike, if it comes. As he gains more experience, he will realize that the strike WILL COME (or, at least, he must believe it will come) and that, furthermore, it will come WHEN THE FLY IS IN THE STRIKE ZONE. He primes his reflexes to strike in the moment when the fly sinks down to that imaginary snout. After more days on the stream, the nymph fisherman begins to "call his shots." He knows that the strike is coming NOW and he strikes almost before the strike indicator does its indicating.

How the striking is done is an important element in determining the success rate of the nymph fisherman. In general, do not simply raise the rod tip skyward. This will move the fly line upward into the air, but not necessarily *along* the surface of the water. The objective, after all, is to move the *hook* into the flesh of the fish's mouth. This is best done by moving the fly line *through* the water, not up off of the water. To accomplish this, drive the tip of the rod toward the bank when you strike. To visualize this, look again at the diagrams, especially Diagram 2 above. If the strike comes early, at the upstream end of the strike zone, your fly line will still be upstream of your body at a fairly right angle to the fly itself. In this position (position 1 in the diagram), drive the rod tip to the bank (the right bank in the diagram) -- but keep the rod tip at the same low level it was in while you were "following" the fly in its downstream path. Do not raise the tip of the rod above waist level as you complete the strike; strike sideways, not up.

The vast majority of strikes will come as the fly seems to enter the downstream half of the strike zone. By this time, you should have moved the rod tip downstream in corresponding fashion so that now, instead of the fly line extending at a right angle from you to the fly, the fly line should be somewhat *downstream* of the fly's location. Look at Diagram 2 again and envision your rod tip, line, and fly being in position 2 or 3. This is *Prime Time* (with apologies to Deion Sanders, the old Cowboys' cornerback).[7] This is when the majority of strikes will

---

[7] During his playing days, Sanders name was usually spelled "Saunders", but his recent biography uses the spelling "Sanders."

occur using the right-angle method. Be prepared. You are fishing over fish (if you've chosen your water properly), you have achieved a drag-free float right down to the fish's snout, you have the right amount of weight on the tippet, the tippet is the right size and length, the leader/tippet combination is the right one, the strike indicator is the right distance from the fly, and you are using the right nymph imitation. The strike will come.

So, begin to set the hook as the fly enters Prime Time. That is, envision the path your rod *tip* should follow (a path toward the bank to your left in the diagram, on your side of the creek). Envision how this path should always be at or below waist level. Then, when the strike indicator seems to hesitate -- move the rod tip along the path you have envisioned. In Diagram 2, when the strike comes at rod position 2 you will be striking almost straight upward; at position 3, you will be driving the tip of the rod low across the water, across your chest to the left, toward the bank. See Diagram 3 next.

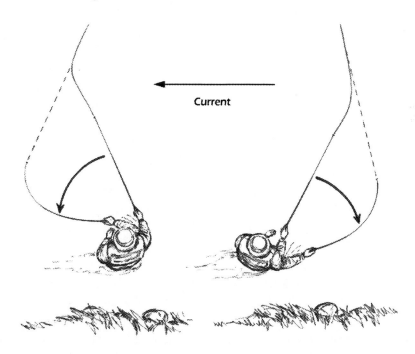

DIAGRAM 3 -- Drive the rod tip low and to the bank (across your chest when to the left).

The movement of the rod (the "strike") should be lightning quick, but gentle. I have taken to watching other fishermen strike, both nymph fisherman and dry fly users, and I see vast differences across fishermen. Some folks seem to waste a lot of motion, always striking upward and not moving the fly line *through* the water. And some folks seem to strike slowly, moving their rod tip through an arc that seems to take several tenths of a second longer than optimal. I once watched a videotape of me striking a spring creek fish -- it was a documentary on the use of non-toxic split-shot -- and I was taken by how violent and unexpected the setting of the hook seemed to be, even though I knew it was coming. Yet, in that film, as for the vast majority of my nymphing on the spring creeks, I was using 7x tippet. That was back in the early 1990's. Now, most of my spring creek nymphing is done with the new forms of 8x!!

I know how this sounds. You're thinking, "Wait a minute, I broke off several fish my last trip out, and I was using 6x. Who is this guy kidding?" Hopefully, no one. I have kept careful track of the importance of tippet diameter when nymphing the spring creeks. The difference between 7x and 6x, using the same flies, the same leader construction, the same amount of weight, the same hatch conditions, translates into an improvement of 50% to 100% in number of hookups when using 7x instead of 6x!! Using 8x improves the number of hookups by another 25% so. And once hooked, you should lose the vast majority of your fish -- on 7x or 8x -- not by the tippet breaking but by the hook pulling out (this will happen on about 30-40% of your hookups even when you are being careful about landing the fish). Later on, we will discuss the prime importance of using 8x in certain circumstances during late July through September, when the fishing is the toughest (and possibly the most rewarding).

There is no easy way to learn how to strike quickly, almost violently, yet softly enough to protect a 7x or 8x tippet. Of course, you have to learn how to use a slip-strike -- the act of holding the line loosely enough in your line hand so that, when striking, the line slips through the guides rather than being held firmly in the hand. I like to tell the story of how my good friend and fishing buddy, Bob Berls, "remembered" how to slip-strike. The year was 1978, during Bob's very first trip to fish the Rockies. After a couple of days catching the post-spawn cutthroats on Buffalo Ford, we headed for Armstrong's. We were sharing a rod that day and I was first up, during the PMD hatch, on the third riffle upstream from the parking lot. We were using the upstream nymphing tactic that will be discussed in the next chapter, and the riffle's rainbows were being extremely cooperative. Back in those days, 5x tippet was the order of the day, and after a couple of quick fish I handed the rod to Bob. On two successive casts he set the hook as the tip of the fly line was moving upstream, with the result being two lost pheasant-tails and a couple of huge swirls as the fish attempted to get rid of the offending hook. By the third cast, Bob remembered this thing called a slip-strike, and by then he had gotten his adrenaline under sufficient control to nail the next several fish and bring them to net. But this sort of thing happens all the time. Every spring, during our first day on the creeks, using 7x, I break off the first couple of fish on the strike. Every year, first day, like clock-work.

It also helps to have a full-flex rod, not just one with a soft tip (Suzanne and I use Winston rods exclusively on the spring creeks and the spring lakes of Paradise Valley and, no, this is not a paid endorsement).[8] But more important than rod construction is line size. I believe that tippets break because of the inertia associated with the floating fly line. The thicker the fly line the heavier it is, and the greater is the friction between it and the surface film. You often see fishermen hold their rods above their heads when playing a fish. This is to keep as much of the fly line off the water as possible, so it does not "drag" and break the tippet. On the strike itself, however, you are trying to move the fly line <u>through</u> the water, driving your tip low across the surface and toward the bank. Fly line weight at this stage is critical. It took me a full season to learn how to use a 3-weight on the spring creeks instead of a 4-weight, and another whole season how to use a 2-weight well, and it has made all the difference. During the early 2000's we switched to 2-weights, and we have been there ever since. Indeed, I simply could not fish 8x during August without the 2-weight rod, and I am now learning how to fish a 1-weight (yes, there is a 9x and its day may be coming, but hopefully not any time soon). "Learning" is the right word in this context, because casting a weighted nymph with a 2-weight in the infamous Paradise Valley winds is a thing to behold and, often, to laugh at. You must be very patient and not abandon the technique simply because you get the leader, tippet, and line wound around your head on every third cast.

Learning to use the "right-angle" nymphing technique, or any of the techniques in the following chapters, means not only learning to envision the attitude of the line in relation to the

---

[8] For over a decade now, we have used an 8½ foot Winston 3-weight loaded with a 2-weight line. It took a while to learn how to cast the 2-weight accurately with long leader/tippet combinations in the Paradise Valley wind, but it was worth it. For the record, please know that Winston no longer makes this basic 8 1/2 foot 3-weight in a 2-piece configuration, but you can still get essentially the same rod in a 3-piece configuration.

"strike zone", but also to make the cast with a light, long tippet on a 2 or 3-weight line. This use of light lines, especially in the wind, is seen as a problem by most spring creek beginners. But the problem is that their casting stroke is too slow and much better suited for casting longer amounts of fly line. Think about this for a moment and let it sink in. The way to minimize drag on the spring creek is to get close to the target and cast a short line. You should move your body to a closer casting position, not cast a longer line, whenever the fish is more than 30 feet away. Twenty feet is about the optimum distance. With a 12 foot leader/tippet combination and an 8 foot fly rod, this means that, at twenty feet, you would have no line showing through the tip top, if there were no S-curves in your line or leader. As a practical matter, the most effective spring creek fishing is done with 10 to 20 feet of fly line showing through the tip top, hardly ever more. Try this. Stand on your lawn and strip exactly 15 feet of fly line past the rod tip. Now, start the cast and memorize how much of the fly line is showing past the rod tip. Now ask yourself how much is usually showing when you are casting your dry fly in actual battle conditions on most creeks or rivers. You rarely cast, in actual conditions, with that little line out, right? Learn how to cast shorter, but with extreme accuracy, even in a moderate wind. Practice this one skill over and over again and you will be well on your way to conquering the terrors of the spring creeks.

The idea is that, with an amount of fly line that is generally not much longer than the leader, the caster must develop higher tip speeds to drive the fly to its destination. At times, this involves more of a wrist action than a forearm action. But such a cast generally cannot be accomplished, except in the complete absence of wind, with a slow, classic casting stroke. For years, I wondered why I never got more than one season out of my 3-weight fly line before it became too cracked to use. I tried switching brands and types of floating fly line and the result was always the same. I am now convinced that these fly lines do not stand up to spring creek fishing because of the excessive tip speeds (coming close to "cracking the whip"). However, $50 or so each year for a properly handling fly line is not too heavy a tab when compared with the rewards associated with fishing these waters and catching lots of fish. Don't sweat the details, for now just try to visualize the process (and the diagrams) discussed in this chapter.

So, now we have covered the first of the several techniques -- the right-angled weighted nymph. As your skills improve, you will begin to NOT differentiate the "right angle" weighted nymph method from the "upstream" weighted nymph – every type of cast will become a minor variation of other types of cast. But, as those skills sharpen, you will begin to focus on:

a) Being accurate with your casts.

b) Making each accurate cast to a perfectly envisioned spot upstream of a perfectly envisioned strike zone or Prime Time.

c) Sensing when the fly is actually entering the strike zone and "preparing" your rod tip to begin its optimal path on the strike.

d) Driving the rod tip in its most efficient direction and in the quickest time when the strike indicator (whether it be the floating fly line or a real strike indicator or the place where the tippet enters the water) does its indicating.

e) Using a slip-strike so as not to break off the light tippet.

f) Deciding when you should change fish-targets, nymph depth, nymph type, distance of the indicator from the fly, or other terminal tackle choices. These last decisions will be discussed extensively in later chapters.

5. The Upstream Weighted Nymph.

The experienced spring creek fisherman will choose his weapons based on what he sees (and, in at least one circumstance, what he hears). Suppose you see no evidence of rising fish. It matters not that there may be real live insects floating down the surface. If you see no rises, not even any bulging rises (which we will discuss later), you are probably wasting your time by using a floating imitation, be it dun or floating nymph. Spring creek trout are not like their less mannered freestone cousins. The trout of Paradise generally will not rise to an artificial floater if they have not been rising to naturals. So don't waste your own time by blind-casting the dry fly. Yes, such blind-casting will fetch a few strikes during the day, but these strikes will come from fish at the "tail" of the probability distribution. These are the really dumb ones, and by mid-June, very few dumb ones are left in the creeks.

But, having eliminated the surface imitation as your tactical choice, which sunken nymph tactic will you use -- the weighted right-angle tactic discussed in the preceding chapter, the upstream weighted nymph tactic discussed in this chapter, the sight-fishing tactic discussed in the chapter after-next, or the un-weighted, "slightly sunken" nymph discussed even later? As your skills evolve, you will no longer think in terms of these choices of tactics, but for now, the tactical question is – should I switch from the sunken nymph or should I go to an un-weighted nymph higher in the water column? The answer depends on whether you can see good numbers of "elevated" fish -- fish that appear to be feeding within a foot or so of the surface, moving right and left to intercept unseen, drifting nymphs. Elevated fish that you can see are often the easiest to take of the spring creek fish, because you can observe their every move, whether they are moving to take any surface flies whatsoever, whether they are willing to move one, two or even three feet away from their holding position, when they open their mouths, even whether they masticate (chew) once, twice or three times when taking an insect. We will discuss specific tactics for elevated fish in later chapters. For now, the question is when to use a <u>weighted</u> nymph tactic, and the simple answer is *when you can see few risers and few elevated fish*. If the day is overcast and there is a glare on the water, do not fret over your inability to see elevated fish. *If there is a complete absence of visibly rising fish, there is likely to be an absence of elevated fish.* So look for the risers and if you see none or only a couple within your field of view, then look for elevated fish. If you can see none, for whatever reason, your choice of tactics is made for you. Go to the weighted nymph. If it turns out that the weighted nymph doesn't work, then it means that many fish are indeed elevated and you simply couldn't see them because of the glare.

Of the two weighted nymph tactics discussed in this book, the upstream weighted-nymph is, by far, the more killing tactic. It is also the weighted-nymph tactic you will use the most, for this same reason. One of the main elements contributing to its effectiveness is that it is simply easier to achieve a relatively long drag-free float when casting the fly straight upstream (or nearly straight upstream). The fly line, leader, and tippet are all coming back downstream toward you at the same rate of speed. There is no need for making a "reach cast" or mending line.[9] You simply need to retrieve excess fly line at exactly the speed of the current. In effect, the upstream tactic results in a longer strike-zone! There is more time on each cast when the fly will be moving straight along the bottom, presenting itself to any fish within this elongated strike zone.

But do not let the benefits of a long, drag-free float, lull you into making long upstream casts. While you may be able to achieve a long drag-free float, your ability to detect a strike and react properly to the strike are lessened the further is the fly away from your rod tip. Furthermore, spring creek trout, even those feeding on the bottom, are susceptible to being lined. You need to keep only the leader and tippet upstream of the trout; no portion of the fly line should land upstream of the strike zone. So remember to move your *body* upstream in order to reach each new strike zone, rather than making long upstream casts to each new zone. Keep your casts within the 20 foot category, not the 30-40 foot category.

Another reason why upstream nymphing is so deadly is the phenomenon of "auto-hooking." The current is constantly bringing the fly, the leader, and the fly line in a straight line back to

---

[9] In general, "mending line" on the spring creeks is a bad idea. Remember, these are short casts. If there is enough line on the water to be mended, then you have too much fly-line out through the guides of your rod. This is NOT THE MADISON. Get closer to the fish. A reach cast or a hook-cast is fine, but after the fly hits the water, any attempt to mend will generally only produce some drag sooner than it might otherwise occur – drag that will be off-putting to your target fish or any other fish in the near vicinity. Rather, learn to live with short, drag-free floats, and learn to raise the fly up off the water (gently) when it has reached the end of this short drag-free float. Don't wait until drag is obvious at the end of the float.

you. When the trout takes the nymph, the inertia of the fly line serves to drive the hook into the corner of the fish's mouth. Even if the trout detects the fraud upon clamping down on the fly, he may not have time to react and spit out the fly before the force of the current drives the hook home. I estimate that, during the early part of the season, perhaps one in five strikes results in auto-hooking. In this circumstance, it even helps to use a larger than normal strike indicator. The more mass and surface area of the indicator, the more its downstream motion will serve as a "sea-anchor," driving home the hook. Indeed, some of the guides use very large indicators not just so that their clients can see the indicator, but also because of this auto-hooking phenomenon. Of course, as in all spring creek fishing, it helps to maintain a very sharp, barbless hook, to help with penetration.[10]

It is with the upstream nymphing technique that the angler will most often experience the so-called "vicious strike." Trout, of course, do not take real nymphs in "vicious" fashion. Watch them sometime and you will see that they time the interception almost perfectly with very little need to accelerate as they would when chasing a minnow. Even the most vigorous swimmers of the spring creek mayflies -- the genus *Baetis* -- tend to swim vertically in the water column, not across the current. At times, therefore, you will see a trout accelerate upward; less often will he accelerate sideways. The "vicious" strike comes when the trout has been auto-hooked and is starting to swim away -- usually upstream, away from the offending hook that is being pulled into its mouth in a downstream direction by the current. In an early (1980) article in *Fly Fisherman*, I wrote that we used 4 x tippets because of the "vicious" strikes of the trout. The real reason was less dramatic. Back then, the trout were less sophisticated, under less pressure. So they tended to masticate longer before rejecting the artificial. Most of the "strikes" came as we saw the end of the fly-line (in the days before wide-spread usage of indicators) moving

---

[10] The barbless hook results in both a higher hookup rate and in fewer lost fish. I have tried both ways and there is a clear superiority to the barbless hook. Apparently, with barbed hooks, some strikes will result in the hook "hanging" in the mouth of the trout, driven only up to the point of the barb, but not beyond it. If the barb doesn't fully sink home, the trout will throw the hook on its first jump or its first head-shake. With a barbless hook, and proper striking method, the hook will be driven home all the way to the bend. In such circumstances, it is difficult to lose fish, even by throwing slack in the line. Most lost fish occur because the trout gets downstream of the angler (who fails to supply a sideways pressure), and the hook pulls through the thin membrane to which it is attached. When you lose a fish in this manner, check the hook to see if some white membrane is attached. This happens most often when using downstream techniques (and there is little chance to set the hook into the corner of the trout's mouth).

away upstream. We had to lift the rod tip to keep contact with the trout, but the current had already done our dirty work for us, auto-hooking the fish. Now, at the turn of the new century, the trout strike "viciously" only in the spring, when they are still relatively uneducated. As the season progresses, they make their swallow-or-spit decision a lot quicker, chewing exactly once. When their mouth opens the second time it is to eject the artificial. I have hidden along the bank in August and watched elevated trout intercept an artificial nymph and reject it -- literally spitting it out -- without moving a strike indicator placed 12 inches up from the fly!

Let's turn now to the construction of terminal tackle. The chapter will conclude with some tips on using the upstream weighted nymph tactic and will set the stage for making the move to "sight-nymphing."

Whether it is the "right-angle" method of the previous chapter, the upstream method of this chapter, or the sight-nymphing method of the next chapter, the spring creek angler must think carefully about the construction of the leader-tippet combination, the right amount of weight to place on the nymph, the distance from the nymph to the strike indicator, and the size and shape of the indicator. The chief difference between spring creek nymphing and, say, fishing the Madison, is that the construction of these elements -- leader, tippet, fly profile, weight, and indicator -- results in a much more delicate presentation on the spring creek, something more closely akin to dry fly fishing than what we usually think of as "nymphing." In a 1993 article in *Fly Fisherman*, I referred to the type of rig I am about to describe as "the delicate nymph" -- and I think such a name is quite appropriate.

Let's begin with the leader/tippet combination. The key to success is to envision what makes a good dry fly leader, then modify it only slightly by making the tippet somewhat shorter, when weighted-nymph fishing, than in dry fly fishing. But hear this: Whether dry fly fishing or nymph fishing the spring creeks, your tippet must be *much longer* than the typical leader/tippet combination seen in books and articles. We'll get to the "why" in a little while.

For most of my fishing I use slightly-modified knotless leaders. Let's say it's the middle of June. There is no need for using 8x, but I know that using 7x will result in a much larger number of hookups than if I used 6x. So I buy a commercial brand of 9' 7x leader (Climax, Umpqua, Orvis Super Strong, and Dai-Riki are all good brands; still others I have not tried are known to work well). I normally keep an 18" section of stiff butt attached to the fly line with a nail knot. The permanent butt section is approximately 0.18" diameter -- usually 20 lb test clear Maxima™ (which has a 0.17" diameter). The store-bought 9 foot leader is taken out of the package and about 18" of the butt is cut off, in order to make the resulting diameter of the leader butt approximately the same diameter as the permanent butt attached to the fly line. Next, I cut off about 12" of the tippet end of the store-bought leader, bringing its diameter to approximately 5x (0.06"). To this I tie a "transition section" of 6x about two feet long. Now, the butt/leader/transition taken together is 10 feet long. The tippet itself is 7x -- and either three feet long or five feet long, depending on whether I am using a weighted nymph or a surface/sub-surface technique. In other words, if a split shot is going to be placed on the tippet, I want the tippet shorter than in "dry fly" mode, so that the hook and split-shot do not become entangled with each other or with the strike indicator. If a weighted nymph is being used, the whole rig is about 13 feet long; if an un-weighted fly is being used, the whole rig is about 15 feet long. The only difference is in the tippet length.[11] And when it comes to fishing a surface imitation, the longer the tippet the better. More on this later.

Now the fly. What fly? What size? The answer will, of course, depend on the situation. But well more than half of my spring creek nymphing is done with either an olive or natural pheasant tail, tied sparsely, with fine gold wire ribbing instead of copper ribbing. Later on, we will discuss fly construction and how this fits in with your knowledge of the spring creeks' insects. But for now, and for the next couple of chapters, let's use the pheasant tail. Let's make it a size 18, say, about mid-way in size between what's needed for the Pale Morning Dun and the Sulphur, hatches that might both occur on the same day during the latter part of June and the first part of July.[12]

---

[11] In recent years, I've been using a 3-foot transition section and the 5 foot tippet in dry-fly mode. This means that I'm using a 16 foot butt/leader/transition/tippet on a 2 weight line. This requires lots of casting practice. Also, the last two years I've learned that there are more and more highly competent fishermen on the creeks earlier in the season. So I've been going to 8x from the get go, as early as April. Nevertheless, don't use my own leader/tippet formula if it does not suit your casting style (or the style I think you should learn and which is discussed later). Rather, simply lengthen your tippet by about a foot for spring creek weighted-nymph fishing, and by 2 feet or so for spring creek *surface* fishing or slightly-sunken nymph fishing.

[12] Hook size really is different from fly size. Lee Kinsey and I, after education from Al Troth, use (for our weighted nymphs) what really is a size 18 long shank but with a size 16 gape. More on this later, in the fly-tying chapter.

The pheasant tail, like all flies used during the weighted nymphing techniques, should generally be tied <u>without</u> weight on a light wire hook (not 1x fine, as in a dry fly hook, but strong standard wire, to withstand the forces associated with landing an 18 inch spring creek rainbow that is extremely mad at you for having deceived him – and to pierce the surface film to help the fly sink to the desired number of inches below the surface). Why no weight? Because I believe that the un-weighted fly moves more naturally in the current. The tippet should be weighted, not the fly, by placing a size 6 or size 8 split shot about 12-14 inches up from the fly. These are the smallest two sizes in common usage. Indeed you will often have a hard time finding no. 8 split shot, except in the fly shops around Livingston and Bozeman (and, I'm sure, near other spring creeks around the country).

There is some controversy involved in placing the weight on the tippet instead of incorporating it into the design of the fly. And I always carry weighted-on-the hook nymph imitations, as well as un-weighted nymphs. Some observers believe that the split shot on the tippet creates a "hinge," which detracts from the ability of the angler to detect the strike -- there is no longer a direct line running from the fly line through the leader/tippet to the fly. I agree that this is a downside, but it is more than offset by two positives associated with the un-weighted nymph. First, by incorporating lead weight into the fly, it is easy to destroy the proper proportions of the nymph imitation. This is especially important when fishing to the multi-brooded *Baetis* hatches. The Baetis are skinny flies, the nymphs being significantly narrower than the Ephemerella that may hatch during the same day. And spring creek trout are selective to nymph size and shape to a degree underappreciated by most anglers. Indeed, it is my guess that the spring creek trout are at least as "selective" to nymphs as they are to duns -- that is, they are as likely, or more so, to reject a nymph based on its size or shape as a dun based on its size or shape. This is because the trout has a clear, undistorted view of the nymph as it drifts toward him. The dun, on the other hand, is distorted by the effects of the trout's "window" as the fly, suspended in the meniscus, floats toward the fish.

Now most of the spring creek anglers are using floating imitations when they witness a clear rejection. During those brief periods of the day when the dry fly anglers resort to nymphs, they cannot observe the fish rejecting their flies. I, however, have spent lots of time lying on my stomach on the bank, spotting for other anglers, and I can attest to the act of rejection when nymphing. To me, these rejections occur at least as frequently as with duns. Also, I see the results of switching nymph profiles to be at least as important as the fruits of switching dry fly profiles.

A second reason for not incorporating weight into the nymph pattern is that it detracts from the angler's attempt to "imitate the wiggle" as Skues put it.[13] In the world of real live nymphs, the actual insect may make several trips to the surface in an attempt to hatch. Each trip consists of a short burst of swimming, then a period of resting, drifting with the current. Even when resting, however, the nymph is being bounced around by the various micro-currents. If the angler is to properly imitate this in-stream drift, the artificial must be light in construction and fished on an extremely light tippet that will not detract from the "bounce" imparted by the micro-currents. It is also important that the split-shot not be placed too close to the fly as some fishermen do -- e.g., within 6 inches. This closeness detracts from the natural "bounce" of the fly in the currents at the depth at which you are fishing the weighted-nymph. Placing the split-shot about 12-14 inches seems, for me, to be about optimal.

The fourth part of the terminal rig -- the strike indicator -- plays another crucial role, along with the light tippet, the delicate nymph, and the light split shot. The strike indicator must be a) small enough to not impede the casting of the rig, b) small enough to not put off any elevated fish that may stray into its path, c) large enough for the angler to see, d) easily moved up and down the tippet to affect the depth at which the fly is riding, and e) easily removed to allow the angler to switch tactics on any particular fish. I have tried everything known to man on this one and have settled on the thinnest widely available foam strike indicator, Umpqua™ Roll-On Indicators (in either red or bright green). But I do not roll on these indicators straight from the package. The result would be an indicator that fails to meet most of the requirements set forth above. Rather, I use a fly-tyer's scissors to cut off a portion of each indicator, using for the

---

[13] It's interesting to compare what Skues wrote with what Sawyer (not much later in time) wrote. Sawyer's nymphs were heavily weighted, usually by virtue of the copper winding built into the nymph. Sawyer's favorite technique, the sighted nymph of the next chapter, involved extremely accurate casting to a sighted fish. Sawyer even used the "induced take" (see below), a method in which he caused the nymph imitation to "jump" up off of the bottom, to mimic the movement of an actual nymph trying to swim toward the surface, where the actual hatching takes place. Skues nymphs, however, typically were light and delicate and floated on or near the surface. The spring creek angler can take the best of both worlds by using a light, delicate nymph, with light weighting on the tippet.

sunken nymph technique an indicator that is roughly 1/8 to 1/16 the square area of each pre-cut square in the package.[14] See photographs. Then I *fold* the indicator over the tippet, rather than roll it on. This creates a cross-section that is low-mass, but still has a sizable square area visible to the fisherman. If, after folding on the indicator, you see that it is still too large, the excess may be trimmed away with the fly-tying scissors. These scissors are so important to me during a day's spring creek fishing that I carry a pair on a D-ring on my vest, with the scissors on its own retractor and with the business end of the scissors protected by its self-cap.[15]

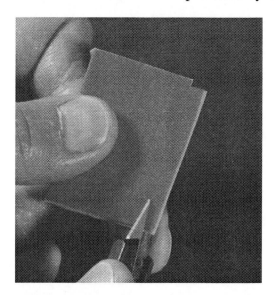

For the sunken, weighted nymph, the indicator should be cut at less than ¼ the size of one of the original sections in the package. Cut off the strike-indicator before you peel off the backing.

---

[14] Be careful. Umpqua indicators now come in two sizes (the same thickness, but with one package having pre-cut indicators that are of a larger square area). Use the package with the smaller pre-cut indicator sizes, or at least the smaller size mixed in with the larger size.

[15] Gingher makes a pair of stainless and plastic scissors that can be stored with the cap on, thus protecting the angler from the sharp points of the scissors. I attach both the cap and the scissors themselves to the vest, so that I can reach for the scissors with one hand and pull it from the protecting cap.

The indicator should be cut somewhat larger than you wish it to appear on your tippet.

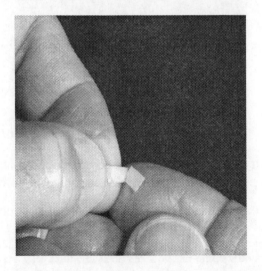

Peel off the back and then place the tippet in the center of the indicator as below.

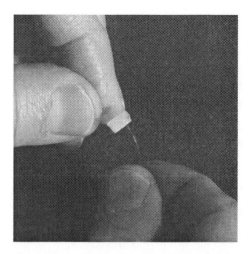

Then fold the indicator back onto itself so that the two sticky portions meet and adhere to each other. Then you can cut off any excess, in order to make the indicator the exact size you desire.

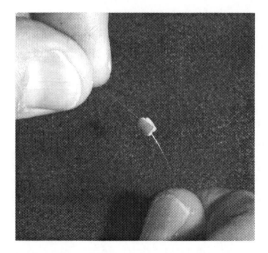

This is the finished indicator, after it has been folded onto the tippet and the excess cut away. The next photo shows, on the left, the size of the micro-indicator typically used for weighted nymph fishing, while the one in the middle is the size typically used for the slightly-sunken nymph technique discussed later. Notice how small are these indicators relative to the thorax area of the size 16 pheasant tail nymph shown for comparison.

The third indicator, on the right, is the micro-mini-indicator that we discuss later on – when the fishing is tough, the fish are incredibly shy of indicators, and you are using an elevated sub-surface pattern but are sight-fishing, not using the indicator as a <u>strike</u>-indicator. We will be discussing fishing by sight, to elevated fish, later.

When using the strike indicator for weighted-nymphing, the size of the indicator should be about four times the mass of the indicator used for the slightly-sunken nymph technique discussed in the next chapter. The indicator should be placed at a distance from the fly that is dictated by the depth and speed of the current -- the deeper the water or the faster its flow, the further from the fly. Lengthening the indicator-to-fly distance is self-explanatory for fishing in deeper water, but for faster currents, this needs some explanation. If you are fishing literally straight upstream, a faster current itself won't affect the indicator-to-fly distance so much as it will affect how much more upstream of the strike-zone you must make your cast. That is, you will need more "lead" time to get the fly to drift down into the fish's mouth. But suppose you are fishing at right-angles to the actual or imagined fish. Then, you will be worried about when drag takes place. By giving the fly more separation from the indicator, you give the fly more room to enter the slower water below the fast-moving surface. To maximize this effect, however, you must make not only a reach cast, as indicated in the previous chapter, but also something of a "puddle-cast" or "stop-cast", which we will discuss later. That is, you are creating S-curves between the indicator and the fly as your rig hits the water. This allows the indicator to float downstream with the fast current while the fly itself is sinking into the slower sub-surface currents. Because such a "reach-and-stop" cast is not easy to learn, I'd advise wading to a spot so that your casts are straight upstream whenever you encounter particularly fast currents (and other conditions calling for a weighted-nymph tactic).

In most weighted-nymph situations, the indicator would be placed about 3 or 4 feet up from the fly. Most anglers make the mistake of placing the indicator way too far up from the fly, often at 8 feet or so. That far up, the indicator stands little chance of doing some indicating. In fact, most times with such a rig, the auto-hooking benefit of upstream nymphing comes into play -- the indicator is indicating a hooked fish, not a strike. Also, up at the 8 foot level, the indicator plays no role whatsoever in regulating the depth of the fly. When using the weighted nymph techniques, you want the fly to ride right off of the bottom, touching only occasionally on the weeds or the moss. If the fly doesn't occasionally tick something on the bottom, move the indicator further up the leader, or put on a heavier split shot, or both. But this delicate nymphing technique never calls for truly heavy split-shot. The angler using a BB or no. 4 size shot is taking himself out of the running in almost all spots on the three creeks, because the fish will hardly ever be holding in water more than about 4 feet deep – and in most cases will be holding in much shallower water. I use only #8 and #6 split shot, with the #6 being used infrequently, for deeper pools during which the fish are not very active and anchored to the bottom.

Now back to the upstream nymphing tactic itself. Start by once more envisioning where the actual trout might be holding in your section of stream. You are wading roughly up the center of the stream, moving to your right or left as circumstances dictate, because you want the casts to be fairly straight upstream. Each cast is made to a particular, imagined strike zone. You "fish out" all casts, even the ones that are slightly off-target. You keep your casts short.

It will also help to "open" up your casting loop. In fact, I find that the technique taught by Joan Wulff, driving the tip of the casting stroke in a canted oval pattern, helps to keep the split shot and hook from becoming entangled with the strike indicator (still another reason to keep the indicator fairly small). In this type of oval casting, the angler changes the casting stroke so that the forward cast and the backward cast are no longer in the same vertical plane. Rather, the forward cast (if you are a right-hander) is made somewhat to the left of the back-cast. You can see from the two drawings below how this helps to keep the split shot from collapsing the cast onto itself.

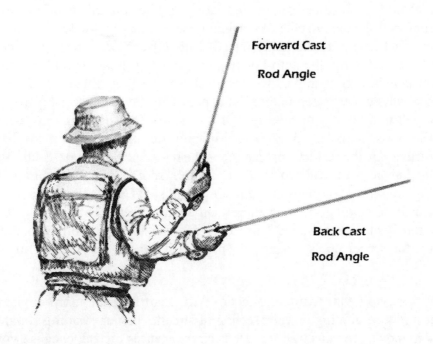

Forward Cast

Rod Angle

Back Cast

Rod Angle

DIAGRAM 4 -- The back-cast is further to the right than the forward-cast.

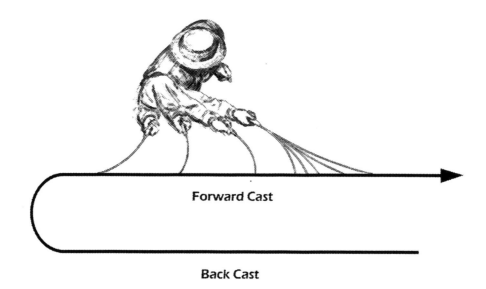

Forward Cast

Back Cast

DIAGRAM 5 -- The canted, oval cast keeps the weighted nymph from tangling with the tippet and/or the strike indicator.

You make the cast to a spot far enough up stream of the strike zone to give the split shot just enough time to take the fly down to and through the strike zone. If the water is especially fast or especially deep, make the cast farther upstream (in fact, you can also vary the distance of the indicator to the fly, and the weight of the shot -- from #8 to #6 – to help in achieving the right combination of parameters). Only by practice and actual on-stream experience will you be able to make these adjustments quickly and intuitively. But the upstream nympher should definitely <u>not</u> keep casting hour after hour without changing some element of his rig, even if the fly itself remains the same.

Now comes the good part -- Sawyer's "induced take." The real live nymph, as noted, makes one or more trips to the surface in the attempt to break through the surface film and commence the actual splitting of its shuck and the hatching out of the dun. As the nymph is swept downstream by the current it will, at times, rise in the water column as it swims part of the way, or all of the way, to the surface. So as the good imitator of nymph behavior you must follow suit. On every third or fourth cast or so, and only once during a particular cast, strip the fly line toward you slightly faster than the speed of the current. Move the fly line toward you perhaps an inch or two more than called for to compensate for the speed of the current. As you can see from Diagram 6 below, when you pull the fly line toward you, this causes the nymph to move up off the bottom and toward the surface. But since you are casting straight upstream, there will be no sideways movement of the nymph. It will rise up, and will continue to drift in a downstream direction at the same time. This slight movement upward of the nymph, while continuing its "drag-free" downstream movement, is what might cause an otherwise unsure fish to strike. You are "inducing" the take, in Sawyer's words.

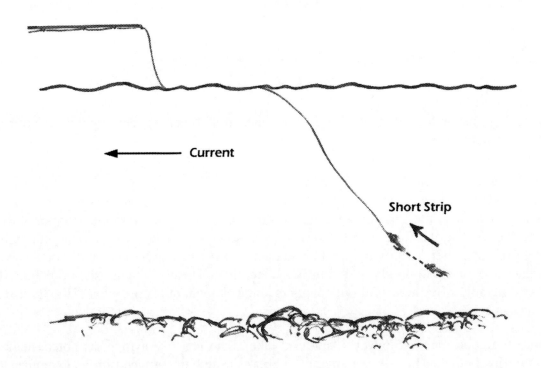

DIAGRAM 6 -- The induced take.

There is a crucial difference between the upstream nymphing technique and the right-angle technique of the previous chapter. When you are stationed opposite the strike zone, you cannot use the induced take effectively. When you are opposite the fish, rather than downstream of it, any attempt to pull on the fly line faster than necessary to take in slack will result in the fly moving toward you, toward the side of the stream, as well as in an upward direction. In real life, nymphs don't waste time and energy by swimming across the current, they only want to swim upward. The spring creek trout know this instinctively and, just as sideways "drag" of a dry fly may result in a refusal, so may sideways movement of the sunken nymph. [16]

Another thing to think about as you are upstream nymphing is the direction you will drive the tip of the rod when the strike comes (remember, it *will* come, and you should prepare yourself to begin striking as the fly enters the imaginary strike zone). Unlike the right-angle method, you will strike generally by raising your rod tip. You can't strike toward the bank when you are facing upstream. You can only strike by driving the tip of the rod in the downstream direction, back over your head. But you should not waste motion, and precious milliseconds, by striking *exactly* over your head, unless the cast is made *exactly* upstream. When the cast is made upstream and to your left, drive the tip of the rod up and to your left when striking. When the cast is made upstream and to your right, drive the tip of rod up and to your right when striking. If you are right-handed, this means that when the cast is made upstream and to your left, you will be striking across your body. Again, proper position on the strike is critical to success. Learn to strike "across your body" when the position of the strike zone relative to your body dictates.

---

[16] Some fishermen might dispute this, since they have, at times, hooked a trout "on the swing" of the nymph. There is also the famous Leisenring Lift, usually meant to imitate the caddis pupa as it accelerates toward the surface. But neither caddis pupae, nor midge pupae, nor mayfly nymphs are programmed to waste valuable energy by swimming *cross current*. When the fisherman catches a fish "on the swing" what's really happening is that the artificial fly starts to rise up off of the bottom at the point when drag starts. If this occurs right in front of a fish's mouth, the trout will take the fly (an "induced take"). But the drag that follows, not the fisherman's reaction, serves to auto-hook the trout – it is this auto-hooking that results in the fisherman seeing the strike indicator (or the end of the fly line) accelerate toward the middle of the creek. The fisherman interprets this as hooking the trout "on the swing" and may even try to duplicate this swing, usually to little effect.

6. Tactics 101 -- What should I be learning on each cast, on each small piece of water?

Now that you've learned the first two basic weighted-nymph tactics -- the right-angle method and the upstream method -- think about one more thing, what I call the "four-cast set."

If I had to name one greatest mistake made by the spring creek angler it would be making too many casts to a particular strike zone (either an imagined strike zone or a visible fish). After the first two casts, the angler's chance of success with that particular fish declines precipitously. Of course, this assumes that each cast is accurate enough to allow the fly to actually drift down to and through the strike zone. For many fishermen, this will not be the case. The trout of the spring creeks maintain especially narrow feeding lanes. I think this is because of the great population density of trout. If a fish strays too far from his feeding lane, he will encroach on another's territory and an "agonistic encounter" will ensue. The observant angler will actually witness this activity several times during the day, as a couple of fish seem to engage in a brief, swirling encounter, with one fish leaving the area and the other remaining. Often, by careful observation you can determine the exact width (and length) of the trout's feeding lane. In the slow water reaches at the tails of pools these lanes seem to be relatively wide, and at times during the day a single trout in one of these areas may range over an area several feet in width, moving great distances to intercept a properly presented fly. But such behavior is the exception not the rule, and the angler should be ever-conscious of exactly how accurate his cast must be to entice the fish. Many times I have observed an angler making 30 or 40 casts with a floating imitation to a specific fish, only to actually hit the target zone on three or four casts. It is these three or four casts that we must be concerned about.

When a spring creek trout sees an artificial fly drift through his strike zone, he must make a decision whether it is real and worthy of opening his mouth and engulfing it. If, during the first time the artificial drifts through his zone, the trout chooses not to take it, the chances are even less he will take on the next drift. And the probability of a strike begins to approach zero on each succeeding drift. The solution for that particular visible trout or imagined strike zone is to do two things -- let the fish "rest" awhile, and when you do return to him, do so with another pattern or another technique. Avoid the temptation to keep on casting to the fish, in the hopes that a better "presentation" will do the trick. You should arrive at the spring creeks with your casting skills at a reasonably honed level. Have confidence in those skills. If the fish does not take the fly on the very first good presentation -- or what you think is a good presentation -- the odds are high that you have a pattern or technique problem. But remember this: *You will have learned something by the rejection of your artificial after only one or two good casts.* Either the fly pattern was wrong or its depth in the water column was wrong.

Maybe you saw no rising fish and, because of glare, could not see an elevated fish even if one were there. So, you started with a weighted nymph fished near the bottom. If you cover lots of hypothetical strike zones, fishing good casts, blind, to unseen fish, with no takes, then cover the same set of fish wish a new weighted pattern (perhaps a different size or shape or perhaps a different order of fly -- midge larva instead of mayfly nymph). But, if your casts are true, and you are not getting any takes (and the rest of your terminal tackle makes sense) you have learned something very valuable: It is likely that the glare is indeed working against you, not permitting you to see elevated (but not rising) fish. But the fish ARE elevated, must be elevated, because your near-the-bottom tactic is producing no results. So you switch to a slightly-sunken nymph, as discussed in a later chapter. The nymph is still fished blind, because of the glare, but now you start getting hookups.

It is, of course, possible that you thought your presentation was a good one, but it really wasn't; there was some drag that was imperceptible to you. This drag was responsible for your lack of hook-ups, not the fact that you were fishing at the wrong depth, with the fly riding below the level at which the (unseen) trout were feeding. In almost all cases, this drag can be cured by *changing your position relative to the trout (seen or not seen)*, not necessarily by throwing a curve or hook in your cast.

So practice the four-cast set. For every strike zone you have defined in your mind's eye, whether to a sighted fish or to an imagined strike zone, make no more than four casts (not counting ones driven off course by the wind or by your failure to practice). At the end of those four casts, always "holster" your fly, bringing it fully to hand. Do this, first, because it allows you to think about what you may have learned about your failure to get a hook-up. But also, you must examine the hook to see if it has picked up any moss. Even when you are using the floating nymph or slightly sunken nymph techniques you will learn in later chapters, the fly will pick up moss. At almost all times during the year, there is considerable in-steam drift of moss and other objects that can foul the hook. And if you have just missed a strike, or the hook actually touches bottom, it is important to touch-up the hook point with a diamond hone. I carry a hone on a retriever and use it after every dozen or so casts. Do you get more than two seasons out of your diamond hook hone? If so, either you are not fishing enough or not using the hone enough, because, with use, the diamond flecks wear away.[17]

So, let's say that you have made your four good casts, and there is no moss on the hook, and its sharpness is OK. Now, rather than making even one more cast to that strike zone, *choose another strike zone (another visible fish or suspected fish) and begin the four-cast set over again.* At this point, you realize that, with the right-angle nymphing technique, the only other possible strike zones, without moving to a new position in the stream, are the ones further out than the first strike zone -- or, you can turn around and fish the strike zones on the other side of your body (assuming you are standing in the middle of the stream). But you must worry about lining the first fish when you cast to other fish that are further out; and, if you are close to the bank, there will be fish on only one side of your body.

It is at this point that we need to develop the notion of a "spatial game plan" for nymphing the spring creeks. Eventually, you will have several nymphing techniques at your disposal -- the right-angled weighted nymph, the upstream weighted nymph, the sighted nymph, the slightly sunken nymph, and the floating nymph/emerger. Each technique involves subtle, and not so subtle, differences from the other techniques. When you first enter the stream -- whether it is for the first time in the morning, or after the lunch break -- spend some time thinking about the stretch of water you plan to fish and how you will use these alternative techniques and,

---

[17] Use a diamond hone, the kind with a small groove for the hook point. Since the largest fly you will be using typically will be a size 16, use the smallest available diamond hone. Larger flies on some waters can be honed without use of the groove. For the small flies, use the groove for the point of the hook, then the flat side of the hone on either side of the hook point, trying to achieve a triangular cross-section to the hook point. Even new hooks should be honed. It also helps to off-set the hook point in a line slightly to one side of the hook shank. Carry a small pair of pliers with flat surfaces, not grooves, on the business end of the pliers. This will permit you to bend down the barb on a new fly. After you get rid of the barb, off-set the hook, then use your hone to touch up the point.

importantly, how you will position yourself, when fishing that stretch of water.

It helps to have in mind a mental picture of where the trout actually <u>are</u> in any, say, 50 foot length of stream bank. In the spring creeks, remember, the trout are fairly evenly distributed, and can be found in, or under, almost every square yard of surface. Let's say you have decided to fish the flat water below the parking lot riffle on Armstrong's (there are literally dozens of similar stretches on the three creeks). It is 10 A.M. in late June and you know the PMD hatch is due any time now. You even see a few fish rising, although there are only a few duns on the water, and you cannot tell at this distance what those fish are actually eating. Pick a spot to enter the stream (it almost doesn't matter where), and, as you are entering, draw a mental picture of where the trout are, or might be, in the area immediately upstream and downstream of where you are entering. If you see even one fish rising in that stretch of water it will help you in drawing your mental picture, since the other trout will be spread out in 3 to 6 foot intervals from the one trout you can actually see. No matter where that one rising fish is, by the way, there are likely to be trout between you and him, so enter the stream carefully and be prepared to fish the water between you and the fish you see. Your mental picture should look something like Diagram 7 on the next page.

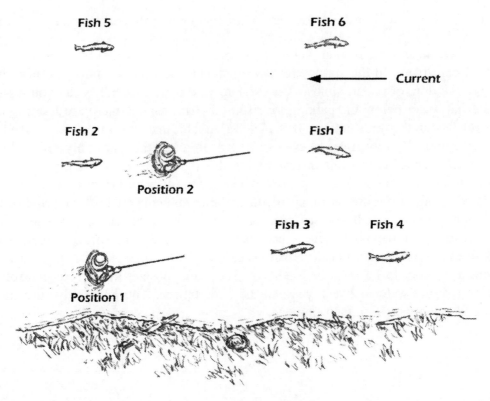

DIAGRAM 7 -- Planning your position-by-position movement.

At your entry point, P1, with you standing only two or three feet out from the bank, the number of strike zones facing you is limited. Your first four-cast set might be to the close fish you have actually seen rise (fish #1). This would involve the use of the upstream nymphing method. But, above all, do not be misled by the fact that the trout has risen. Unless a spring creek trout is a steady riser, you are best off using one of the subsurface nymphing techniques. And even when he seems to be a *steady* riser, as you will learn, he may not actually be taking surface floating insects (including floating nymphs), but may be "bulging" to slightly sunken nymphs, and your technique should be chosen accordingly. So, let's say it is early enough in the day that, you reason, your best chance is with the sunken, weighted-nymph. You have tied on the proper terminal gear, including a size 16 pheasant tail, appropriately proportioned and weighted. You make the first four-cast set *not* to fish #1 (whose presence you are 100% sure of), but rather to fish #2 (a fish you have not seen but believe should be there, in that spot, given your knowledge of the existence of fish #1 and the fact that there is a trout every few feet in any direction of fish #1). You make the first cast to fish #2, not #1, because you know that if you were to cast to fish #1 from the get-go, when you pull out your line from the vicinity of fish #1 this movement might spook fish #2 or at least educate it to the artificiality of your offering. *You always fish first to the unseen fish that is downstream of a known target or closer to you than a known target.*

Then, without changing terminal gear, you might try a 4-cast set to fish #1, #3, #4 in that order. If you haven't gotten a hook-up in those first 16 casts, you might think about changing techniques -- in late June, for example, the *slightly sunken nymph* can be used almost all day with good success, provided you are willing to continually adjust the distance from the strike indicator to the fly -- see Chapter 8. The sixteen casts we've just discussed involve essentially an upstream nymphing technique on fish #1, #3, and #4, but the right-angle technique for fish #2.

Assuming your choice of fly is the right one -- a weighted pheasant tail, let's say -- you must now think about your next position, no matter whether you actually hooked any of those first four unseen but imagined fish. To where do you want to wade? Yes, once you have fished for fish #4 with no success, you might try casting out over that unseen fish #2 to unseen fish #5. But I would strongly advise wading to a new position (position P2 essentially at or slightly upstream of unseen fish #2) before making a series of four-cast sets to fish #5 and #6. *Always get closer to your target, if you can.*

Furthermore, since you are using a weighted nymph, I would not advise trying casts to any of the fish downstream of your initial entering position or any other position you wade to. Save these trout for later, when you can wade in a downstream direction and make downstream presentations to those fish using a slightly sunken nymph or a floating presentation.

Remember Dogma Commandment number 1? "Dry flies are fished across and upstream, wet flies are fished across and down." Well, it's bass-ackwards. You will be fishing the weighted nymph across or <u>upstream</u>, and wading <u>upstream</u> in the process. You will generally be fishing the surface or near-surface imitations in an across or <u>downstream</u> presentation, and when wading <u>downstream</u>. Like anything else in spring creek fishing there are exceptions to these non-commandments. Later on, we'll discuss at greater length the need for upstream casting versus downstream casting. But for now, let's concentrate on the nymphing techniques that are across, or across and up, or just plain upstream.

After you've waded to roughly the middle of the stream, work the water upstream of your position with the upstream technique, as well as the water on either side of you with the right-angle technique. Change wading positions often enough so as to stay within 25 feet or less of each strike zone. This is "shotgunning" in the sense used in textbooks on nymphing, but just like in quail-hunting, don't "flock-shoot." Each of the four casts in a set should be over a specific, envisioned strike zone -- thinking all the while about what you are going to do with the rod tip when the strike comes. If it takes 10 actual casts to complete your four-cast set – that is, if it takes 10 casts to have four casts that reach the strike zone without drag -- so be it. But keep track of the number of "good" casts you are making, and switch strike zones often, and switch wading positions often -- even though you are staying in the same general spot in the creek (in our example, the middle of the parking lot pool on Armstrong's).

Oh, and don't forget to "fish-out" your "bad" casts when fishing blind. Even if a cast misses the strike-zone by a couple of feet, you may still achieve a drag-free float over another trout. So fish the cast out, to its completion. Using these weighted-nymph techniques, about 30 yards of stream bank should be covered in about an hour, depending on your skills. And the weighted-nymph tactics should be used when you see very few rises (and very few sighted, elevated fish) to indicate that the nymph should be fished higher up in the water column. After you've covered those 30 yards, think about going to a near-surface tactic, and/or think about heading back down through the stretch you just fished.

One more thing. When I say "fish out" a missed cast, here is what I mean. On every cast you will have defined in your mind's eye a strike zone. That cast is "over" when you perceive that the fly is dragging slightly or is about to drag slightly. When the cast is "over," you should pick up the line gently and in a manner that does not wave it over other "unfished" fish, if at all possible. If you have planned your approach properly, when you arrive in the middle of the creek, you will already have cast to the fish best-approached from the margins of the stream. So now, and from now on, try to raise the line off the water (for the next cast) in a manner that has the line flying over already-fished fish, not un-fished fish.

When you hook a fish on the spring creeks, you will upset only those fish closest to the hooked fish. It seems that, once the hooked fish races away from its original lie, it does little to put other fish down. And the fish closest to it when it was struck will resume feeding, often in less than a minute. Therefore, it is often possible to hook 2, 3, or even 4 fish, from the same wading position without changing position or "resting the pool." But if you miss a strike or prick a fish, stay away from that strike zone and the ones on either side of it, for several minutes. These fish seem to have some sort of communication going on between them, and the fish that leaves its lie (because you hooked him) cannot communicate with the others near him. I have no scientific evidence for this view, but I do believe that a missed fish does more to harm your chances on nearby fish than if you actually hooked a fish. And while spring creek trout can seem almost dumb at times, do not waste your time on a missed fish *using the same terminal tackle*. Spend your time fishing the other strike zones in the vicinity, then and only then should you retry the missed fish. But it is best to do so with another rig, another fly, another technique.

In the next chapters we will be exploring sight-fishing the sunken, weighted-nymph, then using the slightly-sunken un-weighted nymph, then fishing the dry fly -- including duns, spinners, floating nymphs, and emerging duns. Before we get to these truly killer techniques, you should think about *where* to find actively feeding fish and where you should position yourself relative to these fish. In general, you will be fishing the nymph upstream or at right angles; the dry fly will be fished down and across or straight downstream (this is discussed at length in a later chapter). And you will always try to get as close to the fish as possible -- making sure you've fished out any likely holding spot for unseen trout, as you make your way closer to the trout that has revealed itself.

But where are the fish? Well, this is the easiest part of the puzzle to solve, and yet the part that is the most misunderstood by fishermen. I can usually tell a inexperienced spring creek fisherman. He will do one of two things: a) stay in the same place for hours at a time, because he was told "this is a good spot" or b) he will move way too quickly, covering lots of water, casting continuously, and almost literally stepping on dozens of unseen fish. The experienced fisherman will use the four-cast set to every seen and unseen fish, then, staying relatively in the same place, will try new terminal tackle back over these same seen or unseen fish. Then, and only then, will he wade several feet to a new spot over a new "collection" of seen and unseen fish.

There are a couple of important principles to remember when trying to find visible fish -- those that have risen, those that are elevated but are not true risers, and those that are well beneath the surface but are seen to be actively feeding:

First, understand that with 2 exceptions, the trout on the spring creeks are everywhere. Sure, there are spots where the trout seem to be holding closer together in something looking like a "pod" on the Missouri downstream from Holter Dam. But it pays to think of the creeks as holding a fish *in every square yard of surface area.* If you spend some time trying to see a visible fish in each such square yard, you will be rewarded by being able to use the sub-surface or surface techniques that are discussed next. Remember, your chance of success rises dramatically when you can see the fish, see him move toward your fly, whether sunken or suspended in the surface.

Second, the visible fish will be found wherever two things are *absent* -- a) weed beds that rise to the surface, or b) another angler that has been standing in, or has very recently vacated, an area. Often, I see an angler fishing only the very center of the stream, while ignoring open water only a few feet wide on the bank side of weed beds. Often, I can wade right into the center of these weed beds and get close to visible fish in the open water near the bank. Conversely, I know that I have to wait perhaps 15 minutes or more to begin visibly inspecting the water in the immediate vicinity of where another angler has been standing. But after some period of time, I know that the fish will move right back into the exact spot the recently-exited fisherman had been occupying.

As in any flowing stream, look for fish in the inside corners of riffles or the outside edges of riffles near the bank. But one important thing differs between the spring creeks of Paradise and its free-stone neighbors. The spring creek trout will hold in water too shallow to warrant much of a look on other streams. Often, I will see fishermen on the spring creeks wade right across a shallow riffle section to get to the other side in order to have the sun at their backs. Or, they will avoid a shallow spot at the upstream end of a riffle, not pausing to see visible rises/bulges or elevated feeders. Remember, these trout are everywhere, so as you shift positions, do so slowly and without making much noise. As you take each step, look carefully for new evidence of feeding trout. Then, when you find one, think about what you see. Is the fish taking sub-surface food only, or does he rise occasionally. Make your choice of terminal tackle and choice of technique based on what you see, which might be a very different situation than how you've hooked your last couple of fish. We will be discussing this "conversation with yourself" in a later chapter, after you've learned the other major techniques. For now, remember these simple points:

- There are fish everywhere -- wade and look accordingly.

- Try to ascertain whether the majority of fish are elevated in your vicinity or not. There are several ways to make this determination. First, you may be able to see them if there is no glare or if they actually break the surface of the water with a true rise or a bulging rise. Second, you may have learned that the weighted-nymph techniques are not working as a result of making good casts to good holding water, with a proper distance from indicator to fly, and a proper fly for the time of day and the time of year. Listen to what the trout are telling you.

- Be sure that your rejection of a weighted-nymph tactic is not due to drag, caused by your poor choice of position relative to the assumed strike-zone. Think about what you might need to do to get a better drift -- get closer, change your position slightly, whatever it takes.

- Try to find even one or two sighted, deep-holding fish and use the sighted, weighted-nymph tactic of the next chapter.

- When all this fails (or because you are confident of what must be happening since you can see lots of elevated and/or rising fish), move to the elevated-fish tactics discussed later.

This is the most important message you should have learned so far -- *a major key to your success is figuring out exactly how high in the water column most fish are feeding.* Do NOT think in the manner of most fishermen -- in which they believe they have only two choices, fishing something on top or fishing something on the bottom. This top versus bottom mind-set is everywhere. For example, in Mike Heck's very good book, <u>Spring Creek Strategies</u>, the chapter on nymphing presumes that the nymph will be fished on or near the bottom -- there is no mention of nymphing only a few inches under the surface. Yet a century ago, Skues was experimenting with just such a technique, one we will emphasize in a later chapter.

7. Sight-fishing the Sunken Fly.

My mistake was not in committing the crime, but in writing about the episode. It was the spring of 1980, during my first trip to fish the chalk streams of Hampshire in England, near the town of Winchester. These are hallowed waters, the birthplace of fly fishing, where Halford and Skues practiced their art. Isaac Walton is buried in Winchester Cathedral and the waters of the Itchen flow through the town, while the even more famous waters of the River Test flow through Stockbridge, not far away. I was scheduled to fish the Abbott's Barton stretch of the Itchen. So, one morning in late May, I paid my respects to Sir Isaac in the cathedral, and then walked across town to my appointment with the river's famous wild brown trout.

I had been assigned a ghillie named Bob, a wonderful older gentleman, whose job it was mainly to see that this untutored American followed the rules, the etiquette developed over the centuries since Dame Berners wrote her treatise on fishing with a fly. You have probably read about or perhaps experienced these rules, such as "dry fly fishing, upstream only." To some observers, these rules may seem the product of hide-bound British custom. But the rules actually play an important role in preserving the stock of wild browns. Concerned over the effect that indiscriminate killing of fish would have on these trout, the British, in effect, decided to effectively limit the number of *methods* that the angler could use. The angler must cast only in the upstream direction, for example, and blind fishing is considered poor etiquette -- the cast should be only to visible fish or to known lies. Try fishing under these restrictions sometime; you will realize how limiting the rules are to your success rate. So why not simply practice "catch and release?"

On the chalk streams of the early 20th century, releasing the fish once caught was not an option largely because of the cultural view that fishing was a blood sport and, besides, it was widely believed that, once released, the trout would be difficult if not impossible to catch again. Thank goodness this thinking has changed in recent years. Some of the fishing syndicates that now lease parts of the chalk-streams practice catch and release (of the wild browns, the stocked rainbows are to be killed and eaten).

That day on the Itchen, we were expecting hatches of the Iron Blues and Medium Olives. But real live floating bugs were far and few between. Almost no rising fish were seen and all day only 6 trout were cast to, with only 3 of those making it into the ghillie's long-handled net. The next morning, Bob redoubled his effort to find me some fish to embarrass myself over, but the day started off as a repeat -- no hatches, no visible risers, only a few visible fish on the bottom.

We had, up until noon of the second day, been fishing the "carriers" of the Itchen. On the chalk-streams of Hampshire, miles and miles of canals, or carriers as they are called, had been dug for irrigation purposes and, I suspect, to increase the surface acreage of water on which trout could rise. Over the centuries, the growth of vegetation, along with the natural erosive force of water, had turned these carriers into what amounted to artificial trout streams (much like DePuy Spring Creek in Paradise Valley). Unless you were told that you were looking at a carrier, you would have no clue that this was a man-made stream. Almost without exception, upstream dry-fly fishing is the only method permitted on the carriers. So, without rising fish, your day there could easily mimic my own.

But, on the main Itchen, nymphing is permitted and, after the lunch break, Bob and I walked over to the main stream, which is much deeper with a much greater flow than the carriers. Almost immediately, Bob spotted a nice brown feeding deep against the near bank in a wide pool. I clipped off my dry fly and switched to a size 14 Troth scud -- the pattern that on the spring creeks of Paradise had saved my bacon several times in the past. But now the problem was how to get the scud down to the trout, which was more than 4 feet below the calm surface of the Itchen – a surface that hid a deceptively strong current. I knew that the use of split shot on the tippet was frowned upon. Some of the British chalk-stream syndicates allow weight built into the construction of the nymph, but not the use of split shot. Other syndicates allow only un-weighted nymph fishing. My problem was that almost all my nymphs, scuds included, were built without weight on a light wire hook. As indicated earlier, I do this because, with one important exception (discussed in the chapter on fly construction), I believe it paramount that the nymph, fished on a light tippet, be permitted to bounce and wiggle in the micro-currents, even as the split shot clamped 12" up on the tippet drags it down to the vicinity of the trout's mouth. So, I told Bob what my problem was. Here I was, many thousands of miles from home, with no weighted nymphs in my boxes, and facing the only good size actively feeding fish I might find that day. In an instant, Bob did the gentlemanly thing and gave me permission to clamp two split shot onto the 5x tippet.

The cast hit the water several feet upstream of the trout and I began to mentally envision its path to the fish. As, in my mind's eye, the fly approached the vicinity of the trout, the brownie turned slightly to its left -- and I struck. "By gawd, you got 'im!" Bob shouted, and out came the long-handled net. That fish, perhaps no more than 16 inches in length, had an effect on me all out of proportion to its size. The rest of the day, Bob and I had a blast hooking the wild browns of the main Itchen. At dinner that night with Roy Darlington, the keeper of the Abbott's Barton stretch, the wine was delicious, and the trout of that afternoon all grew several inches in length.

When I got back to the States, I kept thinking about the incident with the scud, and how I might apply what I had learned to fishing the Livingston spring creeks. We began to raise scud in one of the aquariums at our place in the Valley, and the next year I published a piece in Fly Fisherman on fishing the scud and my experience on the Itchen. That was a mistake – for I included in the article the incident involving the clamping of the split shot on the tippet. It is one thing to bend the rules (even under the difficult circumstances I had faced); it is quite another thing to write about it. Datus Proper, my friend and author of the classic book What the Trout Said, had spent a lot of his fishing career on the British chalk streams, and he knew the folks on the Itchen. One day, a couple of years after the event, Datus told me it was probably wise not to ask to fish the Abbott's Barton stretch again anytime soon. I had broken the rules and had then publicized that fact.

But now we are discussing sight-fishing our own spring creeks. The key to sight-fishing, of course, is that first you must sight the fish. This is quite a bit easier than you might think – on the rich waters of the Paradise Valley Spring Creeks. The necessary ingredient is sunlight, at your back. In fact, during the rich months of June through August, when at least two important mayfly species are enticing the Paradise rainbows, perhaps as much as 50% of my trout on any day are caught by sight-nymphing. As you develop your skills and your experience, you will learn to think: "If I see you, I've got you." I am now so certain of my skills with the sighted nymph that I hope for sunny days during the Baetis hatches (the exact opposite of the usual mantra – "Baetis like cloudy days"). While it may indeed be true that the hatch is less dense on the sunny day, my catch rate is usually higher on the bright day.

In the spring creeks, the trout are quite dense in population. This density results from the unusually high amount of food, which in turn results from the constant water temperature and high water quality. Also, the spring creeks don't suffer from spring run-off as does the main Yellowstone River. Because of population density, sight fishing the spring creeks is unlike any other kind of sight fishing you do on any other trout waters of the world. In New Zealand, sight fishing means walking long miles on the bank to spot perhaps a half-dozen fish a day. On other western streams in the U.S., trout will hold on the bottom and rise through several feet of water to take a dry fly. On the bottom, these fish are difficult to spot. But in the spring creeks, many trout will come out from under their weedy hiding spot or their position on the gravelly bottom as soon as the pre-hatch period starts – that is, as soon as the nymphs *du jour* start releasing themselves from their hold on the stream bottom (or the stream weeds) and begin their multiple forays to the surface. Countless times I have stood in a spot that seemed devoid of trout. With no rising fish and no sighted fish, I would contemplate using one of the blind-nymphing techniques we have discussed. Then, as my eyes became accustomed to the light, and as the pre-hatch period started, trout would begin to materialize all around me, moving to a mid-depth position. As I watched, I would see individual fish begin to feed actively. Trout would move to their right or left, often as much as 2 or 3 feet, to intercept nymphs. My blood would begin to boil, for I knew that the next several hours would consist of very rewarding fishing – fishing that would not involve any blind-nymphing whatsoever (if that were my wish). I could simply begin sight-nymphing and could enjoy wonderful fishing, even though the actual "rise" might be more than an hour or two away. Like the dry fly fisher, I could "watch" my fly, watch my fish, watch the fish take my fly, and respond accordingly. I would be sure to catch many trout, while the dry fly fisher did less well, or even went fishless. When the closest dry fly angler would yell down to me – "What are you getting them on?" – I would say something like "A size 18 olive pheasant tail." I could guess that, in the mind of the dry fly fisher, he would be thinking "Oh, he's dragging a weighted nymph across the bottom – yuck." So much for misconceptions.

Successful sight-nymphing requires very accurate short-distance casting -- same as dry fly fishing. In fact, although I'm not sure who invented the term "fine and far off" (it is generally attributed to Charles Cotton) the notion has ruined many a spring creek trip. I often see anglers casting well over 50 feet – as if that's what they were taught in their fly-fishing class. But, since the trout in these spring creeks permit it, the angler *must* get fairly close to the fish.[18] The closer you are the less drag there will be – not to mention the fact that you will be able to more clearly see the fish "moving" to take the nymph.

Still, the first requirement is to see the fish. My friends among the guide community say this is the toughest part -- getting their clients to see the fish. I find the same problem among my own guests, usually accomplished fly fishermen who, nevertheless, have had little or no spring creek experience. When I take such a friend out to the creeks for the first time, I will be careful to choose a good spot to enter the stream. By careful wading, taking several minutes to reach our first stationary position in the stream, I can usually place the angler so that several visible fish are within easy casting range (under 20 feet or so). I'll instruct the angler to simply wait a few minutes, to get his eyes acclimated, before he begins to fish. If I have timed our arrival at the stream correctly, we will already be in the pre-hatch period, with fish actively taking nymphs at all depths. So, after a few minutes of waiting, I'll ask "OK, how many fish do you see?" The usual answer is "Where – what fish?" Perhaps a fish will rise just then, and the angler will say, "Oh, you mean that one there."

The essential problem, I think, is that the dry fly fisher is conditioned to looking for rises, not fish. Even with high-quality amber or brown polarized lenses he will not immediately be able to see fish. This is always my problem during our own trips to New Zealand when, despite all my experience as a sight-nympher, I have had to rely on the guide's eyes for the first few days of the trip. As I get older, I find that I must rely on the guide's eyes during the *entire* trip. Perfect eyesight, however, is not needed – even a person with 20/40 sight can see trout holding a foot below the surface in perfectly clear water (if the sun is behind the angler and there is no surface glare from clouds and no surface disturbance from wind or a riffle). What is needed is experience. This is why, no matter how experienced you are as a fly-fisher, you should hire a good guide for your first couple of days on the Paradise spring creeks. No matter how good is your technique, you will need his eyes until your own eyes are trained.

Now suppose you have passed the first hurdle and can see, say, 3 trout actively feeding within

---

[18] Getting close is also a requirement in the other spring creeks in Montana, including the Gallatin Valley ones. However, in these much smaller creeks, the fish won't permit you to *wade* close -- you must get on your knees and approach them (often from upstream) as if you are a participant in a religious pilgrimage.

easy casting distance of your position. The decisions that must now be made are as follows:

- To which fish do I make my first casts?

- Which nymph should I tie on?

- Should I use a strike indicator and, if so, how far from the nymph should I place the strike indicator?

- Do I need any weight?

- Where, exactly, should I place my cast in relation to the fish?

These are the tactical questions that must be answered in every fishing situation involving a nymph, not just sight fishing. As you gain experience, you will make these decisions without even thinking about them. Your gut will take over. But until you have invested in the necessary number of days on the stream, you can substitute common sense for experience. You must simply not try to rush things. The mistakes I see made all the time, over and over again, by most of the fishermen, including me, are the following:

- We rush to judgment by tying on a rig that has worked in the past.

- We begin immediately to make a bunch of casts – first over the closest fish, then over all the others we see.

- Pretty soon we begin to change flies feverishly, we line fish, we make sloppy casts, and we become increasingly frustrated as our efforts are systematically ignored.

Let's think it through. Again, common sense will help us. Remember we are not using the two blind nymphing tactics discussed in earlier chapters. We are in the middle of the pre-hatch period and we are trying to learn how to sight-nymph. First, develop a simple tactical plan. Begin by identifying the one or two fish that you can cast to without lining other fish. It helps me to think of the stream in front of me as being a series of parallel casting "lanes." Imagine that the creek is made up of 3-foot-wide lanes, maybe 10 lanes in width, like a large interstate highway. Try to use all of your tactical game plan on all of the fish – those across from you, those upstream of you, and maybe even those downstream of you – within the *nearest* lane, before you try anything on any fish in the lanes further out.

You need not worry about what a hooked fish will do to the rest of the "school." Unlike, say, the Missouri River, the spring creek trout do not act as pods. In fact, competition for food is so fierce that rarely does a hooked fish put other fish down for more than a few seconds, rarely more than a minute or two.[19] Remember, the Paradise spring creek rainbows are not shy. They almost certainly are aware of your presence if you can see them. What will screw up the works is when a particular trout, not necessarily the one you are casting to, sees your fly acting in a strange manner (i.e., it is dragging across his field of view). In my experience, especially as the season wears on into late July and August, the truly tough fish can become immune to your offering after only a single instance of a dragging fly. In most cases,, that particular fish is now immune to that fly for quite some time to come. Repeated casts only serve to reinforce the fish's low opinion of you, and, furthermore, serve to increase the chances that a change of fly will do no good. Your aim should be to attack each fish as a single tactical target, and during your attack try to eliminate any instance of your fly dragging near that fish or any other fish. Therefore, once you have picked out your first target, be very aware of where other fish are in relation to your chosen target.

You should try to determine the exact width of the trout's feeding lane. Do you see any instances of it moving, say, 30" to the right? How far to the left does it move to intercept nymphs? These feeding lanes are rarely more than two feet wide, but if your first cast is within that feeding lane, and the cast produces drag somewhere in the fish's vision (i.e., somewhere in front of the trout), you are well on your way to screwing up that particular fish. So, begin by picking your target and learning the trout's feeding lane. Then, learn to NOT CAST. Yep, the key to success is to stop your damn casting. Just stop it! Instead of firing 10 or 20 or 30 casts to that fish, learn to trust in your abilities, especially your ability to interpret what the trout is telling you *on each individual cast*.

---

[19] My spring creek friends and I generally agree that a fish that is hooked and immediately lost will do more damage to your ability to hook other fish than if you actually land the hooked fish. It is as if the lost fish immediately returns to its friends and tells them of the danger, while the netted fish, when returned to the water, goes to sulk over his traumatic experience.

In order to communicate with that trout, you must first be able to tell which of your casts is actually in a position to allow communication. Most inexperienced spring creek fishermen are not adept at making very accurate, very short casts, with long leaders and light, long tippets (in the Paradise Valley wind). I'll say this more than once – *practice your spring creek casting skills well in advance of actual fishing*. The unpracticed angler will find that the majority of his casts will be outside of the feeding lane of the trout. Worse, some of those casts will be to the far side of the lane and will cause the fly to drag across the trout's window. If you miss, miss to the near side so you can eliminate the possibility of drag being seen.

In short, learn how to "erase" a cast. Don't fish out every cast, hoping that even though it missed the trout's strike zone, another fish will intercept your nymph. This might be acceptable practice if you are "blind fishing" the nymph. That is, if you are blind-fishing, missing the intended strike zone may, if there is no drag, properly present the fly to another unseen fish. But now, we are sight fishing. If you see your cast land on the water to either side of the trout's feeding lane, or if you see the fly land too far upstream of the trout, so that the fly is sure to be dragging by the time it gets to the fish's strike zone, *erase the cast*. Simply pick up the fly the instant it touches the water and try again. I have developed a special vocabulary when teaching a novice. On each cast, the angler will hear one of 3 commands:

- "Fish it out" – which means the cast looks to be in the feeding lane and about the right distance upstream of the trout. The angler is to continue fishing the cast.

- "New Cast" – which means the cast has fallen in a place that is likely to cause drag – drag over the target or over another fish. The angler must pick up the fly as soon as he hears my words, and try again.

- "Bring it to hand" – meaning stop casting and bring the fly to hand so it can be inspected and we can re-think tactics.

This last instruction is especially important on the spring creeks when fishing either nymphs or dries. The creeks have large quantities of floating weeds. These are not controlled in the manner of the English chalk-streams. Especially during the heavy traffic months of June through August, wading fishermen will dislodge weeds, which are often seen floating downstream in large clumps. It takes only a small bit of such weed to destroy the profile of a carefully constructed nymph or dry fly. Later on, when we discuss fly construction, we will find that the thinness of the nymph body is critical to success. A single bit of weed can make the fly look all wrong, and it can severely affect the angler's ability to keep the nymph at the right depth or his ability to successfully strike when the trout does inhale the fly. So, the angler must bring his cast to hand often, usually after every half-dozen casts and, sometimes, after *every* cast (when the in-stream drift of weeds is especially heavy).

Bringing the cast to hand also helps the angler keep in touch with how his tactic is working. Simply stop and reassess your results every fourth or fifth cast. Stop and *think*. How many of those casts were truly in the strike zone? Did the trout appear to respond to your fly at all? Did any single one of your casts result in drag in front of the fish? Did you see a clear rejection? This latter case is the most difficult to determine. In the case of the dry fly, a rejection is defined as seeing the trout rise through the water column to inspect your fly. You can see the trout and the fly clearly. If the fish tilts upward to look at the fly, perhaps drifting backward with the fly, but does not open his mouth to inhale the fly, you have had a "refusal." But refusals are tough to identify when sight-nymphing. First, you must be confident about where, exactly, your fly is at the moment that you witness some particular behavior on the part of the trout. This is where casting accuracy comes in. The experienced spring creek fisherman will know where his fly is, within a few inches, throughout the drift. He can't actually see the fly, of course, but his experience, and his strike indicator will help him out.

So, yes, generally you will use a "strike indicator" when sight fishing (we will discuss an exception later). But the indicator is not there for purposes of detecting a strike; it is there for two other purposes: 1) to suspend the fly at the depth of the seen trout, and 2) to tell the angler where the fly is. You will be using a *fly* indicator, not a strike indicator. In dry fly fishing the indicator is the fly itself. In sight-nymphing, the indicator tells you where the fly is – but as soon as your cast hits the water (assuming you do not need to erase the cast), you will be watching the fish, not the indicator. You will see the indicator out of the corner of your eye, but you will be watching the fish. This is because a sighted trout, especially if it is relatively high in the water column, is likely to be quite aware of the possibility of swallowing an artificial nymph with a hook in it. Generally, the higher the trout holds in the water column, the fewer times he will chew on your nymph. The arrogant rainbows can close their mouths on the artificial, then spit out the fraud, without moving a micro-sized strike indicator placed within 6-12 inches of the fly.[20] Speed of strike is also affected by watching the indicator instead of the fish. If you see the fish's mouth open you can start your striking motion before the indicator moves – increasing your chances of hooking up before the spitting-out of the fly occurs.

The toughest parts of becoming a good sight-nympher have to do with a) gauging when the fly is near the fish's mouth (a timing and accuracy issue); and b) learning not to look at the indicator but at the fish. On this second issue – not looking at the indicator – it really helps to make the micro-indicator as small as you can (see next chapter on the slightly-sunken nymph). That way your eye won't be drawn to the indicator so much. Still, you'll always be aware of the presence of the indicator and, sometimes, you will actually see the strike by seeing the indicator move rather than seeing the fish's mouth open. This is especially the case when the trout is across and upstream from you. In this circumstance, I sometimes find that my cast is literally too accurate – the fly sinks down to the fish so accurately that the fish does not have to move left or right. He simply opens his mouth and inhales the fly – but, if the fish is upstream of me, I cannot see his mouth open and I will miss the strike (unless the indicator moves).

The other tough thing about sight-nymphing is gauging *when* the fly is near the trout's mouth. You have to develop a sense of this "nearness" in order to prep your mind to see an indication that the fish has eaten the fly. Once you know that the fly is in a position to be eaten, it is often relatively easy to see some indication that the fish has indeed taken the fly. The literature is full of such indications. Skues called it the "brown wink" under water. Or, simply, the fish turns quickly a few inches to the right or left. Or, the fish "quickens" – his body seems to twitch quickly. Or, if the fish is somewhat downstream of your position, you can actually see the mouth open (which is what we think Skues was referring to by his "brown wink").

During an intense pre-hatch or hatch period, the fish will be doing one of these "eating

---

[20] We have observed this behavior by one of us lying prone on a bank near which a fish is feeding. The caster then puts on a barely visible micro indicator and makes the cast. At times we've seen the fish chew 2 or 3 times without the strike indicator moving, although if the fish chews more than once it is highly likely that the indicator will move and the strike can be detected by observing the indicator. In other instances, especially when the current is slow near the bank where the observer is placed, the trout can chew once, spit out the fraud, and the micro indicator will not even twitch, even if it is only inches away from the fly.

maneuvers" within his feeding lane quite often. How do you know it's your fly he is eating rather than one of the many real nymphs? The answer is that you learn to gauge when your fly is in the "eating zone" – in Prime Time. This skill takes a while to learn and requires lots of practice over feeding fish. I find that I can't do this "eating zone" detection very well at the start of each season and that it takes about a dozen trips to the creeks for me to get really good at it – spring creek fishers go through the same Spring Training sessions as do professional baseball players (the players just get paid a lot more). But once all your skills are sharpened – accurate casts, strike indicator at the right distance from the fly, cast made to the right distance upstream of the trout – you become, as Suzanne puts it, "in the zone." If you fish the spring creeks but a few days a year, you will not likely develop this degree of skill. Still, each day on the creeks will help develop your skills for your "home" rivers, because you will be fishing over lots of trout that are eager to educate you -- and educate you on each of your casts.

A good example of being "in the zone" occurs each mid-season when a sighted fish keeps popping into and out of view due to glare on the water (the dreaded cloudy day). You see the fish feeding, you've chosen the right terminal tackle and the spot to which your cast must be made, you make the cast perfectly, but just then the trout disappears from view. When you are on your game, the clock in your head starts running the moment the cast hits the water. Several seconds later, the clock says "strike", you move the rod tip, and there is now an angry rainbow on the end of your line. We call this a "timing strike." It is literally totally blind in that you can't see the fish and you don't see the indicator move, and it happens more times than you might imagine.

A sub-set of the timing strike occurs late in the season when the fish have become quite used to seeing micro-indicators. Often, the wise rainbow will be seen moving out of the way when the micro-indicator passes overhead, then, when the indicator is 2 feet further downstream, the rainbow moves back into position and begins feeding again. You try to offset this behavior by cutting an even smaller micro-indicator or changing the color of the indicator (from red to green or vice versa), and still the trout keeps moving out of the way. Then you go to your last resort. You remove the indicator, switch to a lighter or darker colored nymph, and make a perfect cast to the right spot. You can't actually see that your cast is to the right spot, because there is no indicator. You can't actually know when the unseen fly is in the "eating zone" because there is no indicator. You rely totally on your casting skill and the clock in your head.

When the clock says "strike" you do so. And when the result is a hooked fish you know that there is no greater challenge to be found on these spring creeks, no greater skill to be learned. The indicator-less timing strike is something we all aspire to, but none of us can achieve consistently – although I understand that Tiger Woods is interested in fly fishing.

Let's review what we've learned in this chapter. The critical keys to sight-nymphing are:

- Learning to see the fish in the water. Only experience will do, so use the good guide's eyes during the first few days of your spring creek fishing.

- Choosing the right fly – a nymph or pupa (see the chapters on the insects and the artificials).

- Determining how to set up your terminal tackle so that the right fly will be at the right depth when it arrives in the strike zone. How deep the fish is will determine weight of the fly and distance of the indicator from the fly – this is why using the Umpqua™-type indicator is so important – you can easily adjust the indicator-to-fly distance by simply pulling the indicator to the right spot on the tippet then re-squeezing the indicator to make it stay at the new spot. *This re-positioning of the indicator can only occur 2 or 3 times before the indicator loses its grip.* If the indicator is "slipping", squeeze it extremely hard for a couple of seconds. If this doesn't work, cut a new indicator.

- Fashioning the indicator – see the chapter on the upstream weighted nymph. But in sight fishing, unless the fish is very deep, you will try to make the indicator very small. Use the following rule of thumb – "If I can see the indicator it's too large" --this is only slightly funny for those of us with failing eyes.

- Truly believing that "if I see him, he's mine." During your formative years as a spring creek angler, learn to stop what you are doing when you see the non-rising but actively nymph-feeding elevated trout. Stop what you are doing, put on the right terminal gear, and practice your sighted-nymph fishing. When you screw up that trout, or hook him, either way, then go back to whatever you were doing before you spotted the elevated nymph-feeder.

- Employing the same casting tactics as in the blind-nymphing chapters. Plan which fish you will cast to first, then try the tactic on another fish, then switch tactics once it's been shown to you that something is wrong with your rig.

- Often, I find that switching the color of the micro-indicator (from green to red or vice versa) solves the problem of the micro-indicator being a put-off with a particular fish. At other times, as indicated above, I go to the indicator-less cast – but not during the early part of the season when my skills are rusty.

- Often, when sight-nymphing, I find that weight incorporated in the fly is preferable to weight on the tippet. I think this is because the sighted fish may have particular restrictions associated with his nymph-eating. It may be, for example, that the feeding trout is in a "window" of glare-less water and my cast to him, to be seen, must be a shorter distance upstream of the trout than would be permitted by a weightless fly. In this kind of case, I sometimes find that the weighted fly will sink at just a rapid-enough rate to put it into the fish's mouth so that I can clearly see the take. If I were to place the weight on the tippet, this might disrupt my "timing" (that is, the distance of only 14" or so between the split-shot and the fly might screw up my timing, both with regard to the cast and with regard to where the cast must hit the water in order to drift into the fish's mouth at the time I can see the fish open its mouth).

8. The Slightly Sunken Nymph.

This is where it's at. As I am writing this chapter, in late January, I know that this coming summer, during the PMD and Sulphur hatches, fishing an un-weighted olive pheasant-tail nymph, a couple of inches under the surface will be my greatest weapon. When fish start to rise – truly rise – to the duns, this technique will out-fish any floating fly I can come up with, including the floating nymph. At this writing I also know that slightly-sunken nymph techniques are widely known, although maybe not practiced as much as they should be. So, I must pay attention to the details.

I wrote my first article about the slightly sunken nymph in a 1993 edition of *Fly Fisherman*, but the tactic has been around since G.E.M. Skues himself in the early part of the last century.[21] The FF article focused more on sight-nymphing than on the depth of the fly, but the point to be emphasized here is that when the hatch really starts and many risers are seen (and almost all the fishermen are using floating imitations) the majority of fish are likely to be feeding on the nymph *just under the surface*. Indeed, the majority of "rises" that you see during the height of the hatch are not true rises to duns (or to "emergers" stuck in the film), but to nymphs just under the surface. The rises are really "bulges" with some portion of the fish's head and shoulders breaking the surface.

In my experience, there are only two ways to be absolutely positive whether a particular fish is truly rising to something on the surface. First, is for the angler to be watching a dun floating downstream and to see the dun disappear within the ring of the rise. If you can see a real

---

[21] "Modern Spring Creek Tactics," *Fly Fisherman*, March, 1993, p.72-75, 90. Skues, of course is the true father of nymph fishing, including slightly sunken nymphs. I don't know who invented *micro*-indicator fishing, although we started to use them independently in the mid-1980's. It simply isn't important who started doing what when (although I try to give credit when I am able) – what is important is to use tactics that result in the fly being presented properly just under the surface. For those interested in the Skues vs. Sawyer literature, it is the case that Sawyer's nymphs were tied with weight. They were continually sinking from the moment they hit the water. Skues' un-weighted nymphs, with hackle fibers for legs, would either float or sink slowly. Skues sometimes greased the leader down to its "point" -- the point at which the tippet began. However, so far as I can determine, Skues never used floatant to suspend all but the last few inches of the tippet in the water.

floating nymph or true emerger disappear, as opposed to a dun with upright wings, your eyes are better than mine.

Second, is for the angler to be facing downstream and to be looking into the cottony mouth of the trout as the upper portion of the mouth rises above the surface. If you see any other portion of the fish rise above the surface except for the top of its mouth, such as its dorsal or the hump of its back, then the fish is NOT taking a "dry fly."[22]

It is tempting to say that the angler should first determine whether a particular fish is really rising before the fly fisherman chooses a tactic – dry fly (including a floating nymph) or slightly sunken nymph. But here are a couple of important facts. During the height of the hatch some fish focus on the dun, while some focus on the nymph. A properly presented artificial dun *may* catch the fish rising to the dun, while a properly presented slightly sunken nymph is highly likely to interest the fish concentrating on the nymphs. More importantly, however, the fish seen rising to the dun will almost always make a pass at a properly presented slightly-sunken nymph. *In other words, if you want to increase your catch-rate during the height of the hatch, fish the nymph straight through the hatch!!*

The technical part of fishing the nymph at the height of the hatch is not complicated. First, you must find a way to suspend the nymph just under the surface. This can be done easily enough by using a micro-indicator anywhere from 6 inches up from the fly to 20 inches or so. The indicator must be exceedingly small because it is so close to the fly. A regular-sized indicator will certainly cause the fish to a) stop feeding for the few seconds it takes for the artificial nymph to pass by, or b) move out of the way of the obviously other-worldly object.

To construct the micro-indicator, we use the thinnest commercially available indicator, the Umpqua brand, which comes in either red or green, as discussed earlier, in Chapter 5. In fashioning the indicator it is critical to cut the indicator before pulling off the backing. Then, peel off the backing and press the indicator on the tippet in a flat manner – simply bend the indicator so that it covers the tippet and re-attaches to itself. See the photographs in Chapter 5.

---

[22] There is still another method. Occasionally, if the wind is nil and there are no nearby fishermen talking, you can hear the "clicking" of the teeth of the true-riser as it takes the surface insect. This happens several times during the season for me, although my hearing isn't what it used to be.

Then, use the fly tying scissors a second time to cut away perhaps one half of the indicator, leaving a flat indicator of maddeningly small size. This takes some practice. And you should have the fly tying scissors on a retractor hanging from your vest. Using your tippet snipper, with its curved jaws, will not work. This is a precision process that you should practice a little bit before heading to the stream. As indicated in an earlier footnote, we use fly tying scissors made by Gingher™, which have a plastic cover for the points of the scissors (and the scissor handles themselves are plastic). We suspend the plastic cover from a D-ring on the vest, and have the scissors themselves attached to a Simms™ retractor through the judicious use of duct tape. See the photographs of an "expert's vest" in Chapter 13 (the Game Plan). When we are done using the scissors, we simply shove the sharp tips back up into the plastic head, which protects us from being stabbed when we need to extract a fly-box from a pocket that would otherwise be perilously close to the scissor points.

In the photo below, repeated from Chapter 5, we show the three sizes of micro-indicator that we typically fashion. All three sizes are compared to a size 16 pheasant tail nymph. Note that the largest indicator (perhaps 1/4 of the size of a full Umpqua roll-on indicator) is not much larger than the wing case of the nymph. This is the size we use when fishing deep, with the indicator 3-5 feet from the weighted fly. The middle size is the actual "micro-indicator" fished most of the day when fishing high in the water column. The smallest of the 3 is less than 1/3 the size of the largest micro-indicator. Use this mini-micro-indicator when there is clear evidence that the trout is sensitive to indicator size, and use it only with an un-weighted, light-wire hook nymph to be fished very near the surface. Place the mini-micro-indicator from 6 inches to 20 inches above the fly on your 8x tippet. When things are really tough, this mini-micro-indicator, fished downstream with a highly elevated sub-surface pattern, will do the trick – the fish will see the fly before the tippet and the indicator. And you should note that I am using this mini-micro-indicator more and more, and earlier in the season that ever.

Macro, Micro, and Mini-Micro Indicator versus Size 16 pheasant tail nymph (on a large gape hook). Note that the largest indicator still is much smaller than a full-size Umpqua roll-on indicator (see the indentations showing the factory-default size of the roll-on indicator).

As noted earlier, you can reposition the indicator several times before having to cut a new one. Also, you should squeeze hard on the indicator every time you bring your cast "to hand" to inspect the hook point -- *squeeze out the water and make the indicator float high.*

At this point in our description of technique a natural question arises. Why go to all the trouble of fashioning a micro-indicator? Why not simply take a realistic looking dry fly and put a dropper nymph about 6-12 inches down from the dry fly? Many fishermen do this, but they are not maximizing their chances. The critical fact is that the actual size of the tippet attached to the slightly sunken nymph has to be small – 7x or 8x, not 6x. Again, don't think this so incredulous that you close your mind on the subject. Yes, you can still catch fish on the spring creeks using a nymph on 6x tippet, but your catch rate will be enhanced (by a substantial multiple) when using 8x. The problem, of course, is that there is no 8x tippet on the market that won't break off easily when it is only 6 or 12 inches long attached as a dropper to the bend of a dry fly hook. In order to use 8x at all, or even 7x, in this kind of fishing, you need a *long tippet* that will stretch and absorb the shock of setting the point of the hook into the mouth of a very angry rainbow trout. So it isn't practical to tie 7x or 8x to a nymph as a dropper fly – since the needed tippet length to keep the tippet from breaking will have you fishing at too great a depth, not extremely high in the water column.

We will treat in another chapter the issue of what kind of tackle, exactly, is needed to fish nymphs, including weighted nymphs, on 8x tippets. But for now, understand only that the slightly-sunken nymphing technique requires the lightest possible tippet -- for two reasons.

First, any kind of spring creek nymphing requires lighter tippets than dry fly fishing (yes, exactly the opposite of the dogmatic view), because the trout can see more clearly an underwater object than one suspended in the meniscus. Even when using fluorocarbon, the knot on a size 18 nymph tied with 6x is massive compared with the knot tied with 8x. And when not using fluorocarbon, the 6x is clearly visible to the trout (and clearly disturbing to the trout after the first few weeks of the season while the creek's residents are being trained to avoid other-worldly things). No less an authority than Vince Marinaro wrote about what the fish sees and concluded that the dry fly is so distorted in the "window" of the surface, that size and shape (i.e., form) and behavior (the degree to which the fly is buried in the meniscus, and whether there is drag) are most important.[23] Marinaro even went on to say that "anything that breaks through the surface film is no longer obscured....Accordingly,.....rising nymphs are extremely well-defined as to color, form, and parts" Now Vince was not in the least interested in nymph fishing, as I found out one day accompanying him and Datus Proper on Penn's Creek in Pennsylvania. But he understood a key issue -- *you have to pay even more attention to detail on your artificial, as well as to your tippet size, for underwater nymph imitations than for dry fly fishing*. This truth flies in the face of what most fly fishermen believe and practice.

A second reason for using the 8x tippet is that it allows the small nymph to "bob and weave" more naturally in the micro-currents just below the surface. The real thing, of course, actually

---

[23] See <u>In The Ring of the Rise</u>, p. 26.

wiggles as it attempts its several swimming trips to break through the meniscus. You can't imitate the wiggle[24], but you can tie your un-weighted pheasant tail on a light-wire hook and fasten it to 8x tippet in order to allow the current to have its way with your imitation. Fortunately, 8x tippet in the form of a strong, flexible fluorocarbon is now available (e.g., G-Max FX) and I now use such 8x for all my spring creek nymphing, including pre-hatch, on-the-bottom, and nymphing with a split shot! Suzanne and I have landed our personal-record 23.5 inch and 24.5 inch fish on Armstrong's and Nelson's with 8x (on 2-weight lines, which are critical). But for the 8x to work (and for you not to be "contributing" artificial flies to the food chain, the tippet must be very long -- at least 50% longer than the typical tippet length in the typical leader/tippet formula. Finally, in order not to break the long, fine tippet on the strike, the fly line itself must be light and not have massive surface area. But how do you "turn over" this long, light tippet with a 2-weight or 3-weight fly line, in the wind? More on this later, but for now please remember this:

The spring creek fishing techniques I am describing represent a true "system" -- long tippets, light tippets, light fly lines, different casting strokes than the typical, classical, slow-timing casting stroke. *Leave out any single one of the elements of this system, and you will come to the conclusion reached by the vast majority of the anglers that have tried to use 8x tippets -- "this is a waste of time."* I spent an interesting day with a good friend on Armstrong's this spring. He insisted on using 8x tippets with his 3-weight rod, and paid the price by losing quite a lot of flies on the strike.

Use of the micro-indicator is another part of the system and it is a huge improvement over the ancient practice of "greasing" the leader. Skues was the first to perfect the art of fishing to bulging fish, and when he didn't use a greased leader he would have to detect the strike by actually seeing the bulging rise. This technique was really an extension of dry fly fishing where the strike indicator is the rise itself. When it was cloudy and he could not see the fish, or when the bulging rise could not be detected, Skues would grease the leader (but not the tippet) and then use the "point" at which the leader/tippet connection entered the water to detect the rise. I have used this technique myself on flat water, where, in the proper lighting conditions you can

---

[24] Swisher and Richards wrote about their wiggle-nymph, which is constructed of two separate hooks. This fly is not tied commercially in very small sizes, and, further, it would be difficult to achieve the hinged, wiggle effect while maintaining thinness in nymphs of very small sizes.

see the point being drawn further into the water by the fish's eating of your nymph.[25]

The problem with the greased leader/tippet technique is a) you cannot easily adjust the depth of the fly without getting into clumsy de-greasing and re-greasing; and b) the greased leader itself will float throughout its length and contribute more to drag than the submerged leader. The thin, small, micro-indicator solves these problems because, first, the leader or tippet will sink on either side of the floating indicator. Second, you can easily reposition the indicator – just pull on the indicator (while it is folded on the tippet) until it breaks its hold, move it to your new position, then press hard on the indicator to reset its grip on the tippet. After several such re-positionings the indicator will lose its ability to adhere to the tippet and you will have to cut a new micro-indicator and start over. You can tear off the old one simply by pulling it at a right-angle away from the tippet (be sure to place the used indicator in a pocket so that you don't contribute to spring creek trash).

The frequent re-positioning of the micro-indicator is an important part of the slightly-sunken nymph technique. First, suppose that the surface of the water has glare and you can never actually see the trout, you don't see its bulges, but past experience tells you that there is definitely a feeding trout in that particular square-yard of surface. You make a cast, perfect in its accuracy, with the indicator 6 inches from the fly, but there is no take. It may be that this particular unseen trout is feeding furiously at a depth lower than your fly is set. After fishing to several suspected lies with the indicator positioned at 6 inches, you can then reposition the indicator at, say, 20 inches from the fly and start over. In either case, because conditions don't allow you to see the fish, you must rely on the slight pause in the micro-indicator to tell you when to strike.

Distance of indicator-to-fly is important for another reason. Some fish become, by mid-season,

---

[25] When using very long tippets, as we do, the tippet might have to be greased down most of its length, to within a few inches of the fly. Interestingly, tippets of the length we use -- to reduce drag and to protect the 8x tippet material -- were unheard of in Skues time and are unheard of today. For example, in Heck's book, p. 103, he shows nymphing leaders that have tippets of up to 26" in length; on p. 126 he shows dry-fly leaders that have tippets of up to 27" in length. By contrast, we never use tippets less than 36-48", and I often use tippets of approximately 60". Learning to cast a rig with such tippet lengths takes some practice as we discuss in a later chapter.

very aware of the micro-indicator, no matter how small you make it. These fish will move several inches out of the way of the indicator before they return to their precise feeding position and intercept another piece of food. For such a fish, you may have to <u>increase</u> the indicator-to-fly distance, not because the fish is feeding deeper than others, but because you need to give the trout more time – after the indicator has passed overhead – to then take the artificial attached to the tippet. Sometimes, under cloudy conditions when I cannot see the fish (and he is not bulging), I move the indicator to as much as 36 inches up from the fly. Then, when I make the cast, I at least have a good chance that the fish will suspend feeding for the seconds it takes for the indicator to pass downstream of him – and the next thing the fish eats is my artificial. Sometimes, the cloud-driven glare on the water comes and goes. In these conditions I frequently use the longer indicator-to-fly distance and, if, at the moment when the fly is supposed to be near the fish's mouth, I don't see the indicator pause, I use a timing strike, as we discussed earlier. The fly ought to be in the mouth NOW, so STRIKE! This timing strike might be used several times each day, with one or two successes. But interestingly, I rarely foul hook a trout, except when I'm using too long a cast and don't have complete control over the process of sensing the strike and driving the rod tip in the right direction.

Remember, you generally want to use a light-wire hook without any weight when using the slightly-sunken nymph technique. This allows the "bob and weave" movement of the artificial. But this also means that when you move the indicator from, say, 6" away from the fly to, say, 20" away from the fly, the result might be that the hook rides 8" deep in the current instead of 2" deep. That is, the depth at which the fly rides in the water column (as the cast reaches the strike zone), will depend not only on the distance of the indicator to the fly, but also on the density of the fly (light wire hook or thicker hook) and the speed of the current.

If I want to keep the fly at the same depth but feel that I need to increase the distance from the fly to the indicator, then I need to *decrease* the density of the fly (by using the un-weighted PT on a lighter, dry fly, hook). See the chapter on the artificial nymphs – we use weighted PTs on nymph hooks, un-weighted PTs tied on nymph hooks, un-weighted PTs tied on dry fly hooks, and PTs tied on dry fly hooks and treated with dry fly spray. There are effectively four densities of fly, several colors of fly, and an infinite number of distances of fly-to-indicator. There are also an infinite number of distances from the cast hitting the water to the downstream position of the fish. Your intuition and experience plays a role in how you adjust each of these variables to give yourself the best chance at getting the fly down to the fish in a manner that will make him want to eat it

You must constantly fiddle with these variables – density and color of nymph, indicator-to-fly depth, and target spot upstream of the fish to aim your cast -- to get the fly to the depth of the fish (or compensate for the micro-indicator-shy behavior of a specific fish). But when you do, the clock in your head (the one that determines when the fish should be inhaling your fly) needs to make the adjustment as well. This is what practice is all about. And this practice – unlike casting -- can only be done right if you are actually on the creek. As in most disciplines, experience really counts.

It is also the case that sometimes, you will want to violate the "rule" of using un-weighted flies on light-wire hooks. I carry lots of weighted pheasant tails tied by Lee Kinsey. He uses a very small diameter black wire to make the thorax area under the wrap of pheasant-tail – see the fly-tying chapter. There are many circumstances when a sighted fish is in a spot when I want the fly to get down to the fish FAST. Often, this has to do with conditions of glare – I can't see the micro-indicator land upstream (in the spot I'd normally cast to with an un-weighted fly). So, I need to use a weighted fly and cast closer (further downstream) to the fish, in order to see the micro-indicator land and therefore track the fly.

9. The Mayfly Hatches – Sulphurs and Other Baetis.[26]

As most fly-fishermen know by now, the spring creeks of Paradise Valley suffered devastating floods in the spring of 1996 and again in June of 1997. A massive, and expensive, reconstruction effort after the 1996 flood was successful in keeping the Yellowstone River out of Armstrong's and DePuy's during the 1997 flood event. Nelson Spring Creek was not affected in either year. The annual hatches seemed sparse or non-existent during 1997, but by mid-summer 1998, hatches on the spring creeks were again prolific and the number of trout was at pre-flood levels (although the percentage of brownies greatly increased due to the influx of river fish from the Yellowstone). And, once again, visiting anglers were being frustrated by the famous "sulphur" hatch in July and August.

Many fishermen are convinced that the sulphurs are the work of some demented angling deity. Typically, fishing will be relatively easy in the morning, as the remnants of the summer's PMD hatch bring many fish up on the surface -- strikes occur both to nymph and dun imitations. But by mid-afternoon, the sulphurs take over the stream. Thousands of trout up and down the creek begin rising as the small, yellow-colored mayflies take to the air. Yet, angler after angler has no success fishing dun imitations. We have studied this hatch intensively over the years -- both from a fishing and an entomological viewpoint -- and here is the lowdown.

First, many anglers refer to the fly using an incorrect Latin name. It is <u>not</u> the genus *Centroptilum*, as had been posted on the hatch-boards of some of the local fly shops. This misidentification has been reinforced by some of the fishing literature (which has never been known for its entomological accuracy). *Centroptilum* is indeed found nearby in the mainstem Yellowstone River, which generally is much warmer in August than the spring creeks. Some of the *Centroptilum* spinners have strayed over into the neighboring spring creeks and have been positively identified; but these insects have <u>not</u> established colonies on any of the three streams. In the extensive general benthic samples taken by Dan Gustafson, a Ph.D. entomologist

---

[26] The first part of this chapter is taken mainly from a paper written by John Mingo and Dan Gustafson that appeared on the www.flyfisherman.com website ("The Sulphurs of Paradise," early 2001). I do NOT treat the PMDs in this book because so much has already been written about them (see chapter on fly recipes).

working now out of Western Montana State University, not a single *Centroptilum* dun or nymph was found in the spring creeks.

The August sulphur, the one that hatches every afternoon on these creeks, is an ordinary *Baetis tricaudatus*. This fly is found all over North America, from coast to coast, as far north as the Alaskan tundra and as far south as northern Mexico. Pat McCafferty, the Purdue entomologist and author of the well-received <u>Aquatic Entomology</u>, believes that *B. tricaudatus* is "possibly the most ubiquitous mayfly in North America." McCafferty has confirmed that the *Baetid* found in the spring creeks in August is *Baetis tricaudatus*, not *Centroptilum*, based on samples I've sent to him.

This fly in many parts of the country exhibits multi-voltinism, meaning there are two or more broods of the insect each year. On the spring creeks in Montana, there are distinct hatches in early spring, again in mid-summer, and again in the fall. But the mid-summer fly exhibits a very different coloration than during the spring and fall hatches, due to differences in water and ambient temperatures. In August, the *Baetis* is no longer the famous "blue-wing olive." Rather, the male *Baetis* dun is a very pale olive color, bordering on tan, while the female dun is decidedly yellow or sulphur in color. It is also the case that the August brood is somewhat smaller than the Spring brood of *Baetis*.

Furthermore, in the samples taken by Gustafson, female duns have outnumbered males during the hatch by about 2 to 1. In the air, both male and female dun look "light Cahill" in color, but only the male, up close, has an olive cast to its coloring. We do not know why the female duns have outnumbered the males in our samples — but there are several possibilities. For example, it is known that some species can lay eggs without mating and it is known that early season hatches sometimes have higher proportions of females. Also, it is possible that the males, for some reason, exhibit greater mortality during hatching or that there are sparser, less noticed hatches of male duns during other times of the day.

Gustafson, examining all three Paradise Valley spring creeks, has determined that, in mid-summer, mature nymphs of only three mayfly genera account for over 95% of all mayflies in the streams -- *Baetis tricaudatus*, *Ephemerella inermis*, and *Callibaetis*. There are also minor populations of *Paraleptophlibia debilis*, *Diphetor hageni*, and *Attenella margarita*. In addition, the Armstrong/DePuy system (but not Nelson's) has small amounts of *Tricorythodes minutus*.

For many spring creek fishermen, it will stretch the bounds of credibility to learn that the "blue-wing olive" and the "sulphur" are the same species! But this phenomenon is not unique to the spring creeks. For example, McCafferty says that some "sulphurs" found in Wisconsin and Michigan are *Baetis tricaudatus*, and we suspect that this misidentification of "sulphurs" as *Centroptilum* instead of *Baetis* has occurred elsewhere in the Rockies as well. Why has the misidentification of this species taken place? Probably, the amateur entomologists have made two classic mistakes. First, color is generally *not* an indicator of genus, let alone species. Don't take anything for granted! Second, the genus *Centroptilum* generally has a "spur" or costal angulation on its hind wing (in fact, the British refer to this genus as the "spur-wing"). But so does *Baetis*. The spur on the hind wing of the *Centroptilum* is hooked, but the spur on the *Baetis* is straight. Further, the *Baetis* has two so-called intercalary veins on its main wing (the small veins between the main veins), the Centroptilum has one. A good quality 8 power loupe or microscope is needed to make these distinctions.

But, the reader will ask, what does all this have to do with catching fish? Well, here are some useful observations, based on our long, combined fishing/entomological experience:

1) *Baetis* nymphs are strong swimmers. Indeed, the Baetidae family is now generally referred to in the entomological literature as "the small minnow" mayfly. This means that motion imparted to a weighted nymph often does the trick. But don't just swing your nymph imitation aimlessly in the current. Also, don't make the mistake of weighting the nymph itself too heavily, thereby detracting from the motion naturally imparted by micro-currents around the fly. Rather, use – sparingly -- an induced-take procedure as described in Chapter 5 (the Upstream Weighted Nymph). The technique is essentially Sawyer's "sudden inch," and it can be a killer during the pre-hatch period.

During the hatch period itself, the slightly-sunken nymph technique will be a killer, except for one important point. By this time of the year (early July) the trout in the spring creeks are becoming truly educated – the "PhD pool" on DePuy's got its name from this hatch on these smart rainbows. It is important to recognize that good fishermen will have been using the slightly-sunken nymph technique for a couple of months now, so you may have to go to a floating imitation (true floating nymph or floating emerger) to get your strike.

2) The abdomens of *Baetis* nymphs and duns are much narrower than those of the *Ephemerella* (pale morning dun) hatching earlier in the morning (see photos). If your pheasant-tail patterns or your comparadun patterns have thick abdomens -- as many store-bought flies do -- you may as well leave them at home during the sulphur hatch. A <u>thin</u>, olive pheasant tail nymph or pale olive/pale yellow thorax dun, both in size 20 (sometimes smaller) are well suited to matching this hatch. (See photos below of Ephemerella and Baetis nymphs – the photo on the left is the Baetis.}

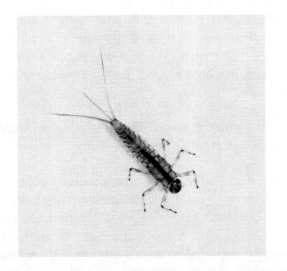 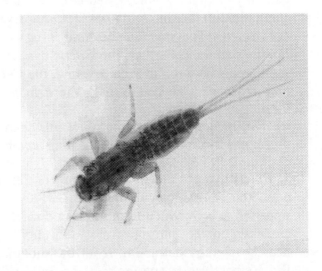

The longer Ephemerella nymph is also much wider, for a given length than the Baetis. The two photos are roughly the same degree of magnification. Notice that the Ephemerella also has much thicker legs. Nevertheless, we have not found it necessary to imitate legs in the nymph pattern, since these are folded back along the sides of the nymph when it is swimming (upward in the water column). Finally, note that the Ephemerella nymphs are usually somewhat darker in color than the Baetis nymphs – so it often helps to use a natural Pheasant Tail or a light olive dyed PT rather than the dark olive PT that is used when imitating the PMD nymph.

3) The summer afternoon Baetis hatch sometimes occurs simultaneously with a *Diptera* (midge) hatch; the midge is generally around a size 20-22. Unless you are willing to switch, and switch often, between a mayfly nymph pattern and a midge pupa pattern, your success will be limited. Also, you must be willing to switch flies and/or tactics *on any given fish.*

4) The angler must pay extra-careful attention to rise-forms. Many trout are quite dun-shy during the sulphur hatch (even more dun-shy than they are slightly-sunken-nymph-shy). They may be "bulging" under the surface. The inattentive angler will think a particular trout is truly feeding on the surface to duns or floating nymphs, and he will waste valuable time using a surface imitation.

5) Finally, many fishermen make the mistake of staying in one place in the creek for long periods of time. Often, we see a caster glued to a spot, making cast after cast to the same fish or group of fish. As we have said earlier, after only three or four well-placed casts to a single fish, your chances of a hook-up become exceedingly low, unless you change flies, tactics, or targets. Switching between weighted nymphs, micro-indicated slightly-sunken nymphs, and floating nymphs or emergers generally is all that is needed. But if you make, say, 10 well-placed casts to a single fish and <u>then</u> change flies or tactics, your chances of success are not high.

The angler who does not fish the Paradise spring creeks regularly, often misjudges the number of fish in the streams and their distribution. The angler, even though he is constrained by other anglers upstream and downstream of his position, should try to move around. Often, a change in position of less than 20 feet will present the fisherman with several new "targets" or better angles on existing targets. The best guides understand this, and they reposition their clients many times during the day.

10. Midges.

The mayfly hatches of the spring creeks receive the most attention in the fly-fishing magazines, in the textbooks, and from some of the guides. The reservation-books of the creeks are filled to capacity during the PMD hatches and the Sulphur hatches. When someone says "I did really well on the surface today," you are likely to think immediately that he means "I did well fishing a dun or mayfly emerger." But the midge hatches of the creeks are at least as important as the mayfly hatches during the peak months of the mayfly hatches (i.e., July and August), and are more important than the mayfly hatches at other times of the year.

I'm not referring necessarily to the possibility that midges can account for a higher percentage of fish food than the mayflies (which they can). I'm referring to the importance of the midge in keeping the fly fisherman occupied with lots of hookups during the periods when mayfly pre-hatches, hatches, and spinner falls are not dominating the feeding behavior of the trout. Every fisherman I know of, including me, usually encounters "slow" periods during the day, when fewer rising or bulging fish are seen, and the hook-up rate of the fisherman declines. Sometimes there will be a 2 or 3 hour dry spell. In June, this dry spell can be very frustrating, especially if a spinner fall does not occur until late in the day (or not until the next morning). It is during each such "dry period" that I concentrate, first, on fishing midge imitations, followed by the fishing of scud and sow-bug imitations.

The fishing of midge imitations can involve just as much dogma as the fishing of mayfly imitations. Let's start with the midge larva. As most fly-fishermen know, larvae are the "first" sub-aquatic stage of the midge, followed by the pupae, followed by the adults. Since the larvae transform themselves into the pupae under the surface of the water (and usually near the bottom of the creek), and since it is only the pupae that, like mayfly nymphs, make the journey up into the surface-film of the water to emerge as adults, fly-fisherman tend to think of larva imitations as something you fish "on the bottom." Since fishing "on-bottom" at the spring creeks can usually only be accomplished by incorporating weight into the imitation, or placing weight on the tippet, that is what the fisherman does. Or, most likely, the fisherman simply doesn't use a larva imitation on the spring creeks – because he or she doesn't particularly like "bouncing a weighted fly along the bottom." Neither do I. *So, it's a good thing that at certain times of the day, midge larvae become quite accessible to the trout high in the water column.*

Rick Hafele, the co-author of the good book -- The Complete Book of Western Hatches (with Dave Hughes) -- has provided some insights into what he calls "behavioral drift." This refers to the fact that aquatic insects have similar needs to land-based animals with regard to food, shelter, protection from predators, and reproduction. In the process of meeting those needs, nymphs, midge larvae, scuds, etc., often move from location to location within the spring creeks, just like a group of deer might move along well-established trails. Unlike land animals that might move back and forth along a single trail in the course of a day, the aquatic insect spends essentially no time swimming up-stream (because it is too energy-consuming) and very little time swimming across stream (again, because it is energy-consuming in relation to the achievement of its goals). Rather, almost all of the swimming time of the sub-aquatic life stages of insects, is spent in "releasing" the insect's hold from weeds or gravel, swimming perhaps upward in the water column, then either a) making it to the surface to hatch (in the case of mayfly nymphs or midge pupae) or b) drifting with the current downstream, until a better location is found (or at least until the insect senses it has found a better location) below the surface of the water (in the case of immature nymphs or midge larvae). Therefore, when you are imitating sub-aquatic stages of insects, it is important to NOT spend time on "swimming" your imitation across current, unless you happen to be using an imitation that reflects, for example, stonefly behavior in reaching the shore to climb out of the stream to molt.

With regard to midges, it is well known that the stage of its life involving the pupa has, as its objective, the pupa swimming to the surface, breaking through the meniscus, and "hatching" into the adult, much as is done by a mayfly nymph. But what is *not* known well is that midge larvae also often break loose of a holding place, swim toward the surface, drift with the flow, then go back down to re-attach themselves to a new holding place among the weeds (which such holding place can be high or low in the water column, depending on weed growth). Hafele has written that in-stream behavioral drift of midge larvae may account for a very high percentage of all behavioral drift. In a study of a coastal creek in Oregon,[27] he finds that Baetis nymphs account for 18% of all behavioral drift and that this is second to behavioral drift of Chironimid larvae at 29%!! More

---

[27] See "Get the Drift", *American Angler*, year unknown, p. 18.

important -- and not mentioned in Hafele's writings, so far as I know -- is that within the Paradise spring creeks, the midge larvae can get very high in the water column when drifting, and can drift a very long way (if not intercepted by a trout's mouth).

This knowledge made its way to me by accident when, one day on Armstrong's in June, the PMD pre-hatch period had not yet started (it was around 10A.M.). While standing there trying to figure out what to do, I looked down and saw, just inches below the surface, several small white larvae, wriggling in the near-surface current. I happened to have in my box some of the "miracle nymphs" used by some of the local guides (which is a name that really should be "miracle larva" not miracle nymph). I put on an un-weighted size 18 larva imitation, with a micro-indicator about 20 inches up from the fly, and proceeded to have many hookups for the next hour until the PMD pre-hatch started in earnest.

Hafele indicates that behavioral drift occurs throughout the day, but that there are 3 peak periods – the time from about 1 hour before and after dawn, the time from about 1 hour before and after dusk, and around the middle of the night. Now, due to my love of sleep, and my desire not to stumble around the creeks in the dark, I typically never fish at these times. Fortunately, however, the midge-larvae-high-in-the-water-column phenomenon occurs almost every day in the spring creeks, especially during June and July. This high-drift doesn't seem to be as prevalent in late summer or early fall, but earlier in the summer it happens every day, sometimes before the PMD pre-hatch, sometimes before the afternoon Sulphur pre-hatch, and sometimes during both periods. Perhaps this larva-drift is simply there all during the day (at levels below Hafele's three peak periods), and I simply notice it more when there are no pulse-quickening mayfly activities. In any case, the white midge larva imitation is a big weapon in my arsenal. It seems to be especially effective on the smart feeders that choose to take up very shallow lies, at the edge of the riffles and at the extreme edges of pools, close to the bank. For this kind of fishing, 8x tippet, an exceedingly small "mini" micro-indicator, and accurate casting with an un-weighted larva imitation are crucial to success. The chapter on tying the imitations gives a recipe for the white "miracle nymph."

Now let's move to the midge pupa. The midge pupa imitation is well known by the crowd at the spring creeks. Everyone has several "flavors" of imitation – variants of the brassie, variants of goose-biot-bodied pupae, colors ranging from black to bright red, and sizes ranging down to size 22 or size 24. We'll discuss this in more detail in the chapter on tying imitations. The key point to keep in mind is that midge pupae imitations are one of the very most important tools for success even during the mayfly halcyon days of June and July – and midge pupae are absolutely critical for success during the early March-April-May days, when midge hatches seem to outweigh mayfly hatches in volume and even in size of the real insect. During March especially, the midges of the spring creeks seem to be on the order of a size 16 – and I always seem to be cursing myself for not having enough of those larger sizes in my box.

In my experience, I find that thinness of the larva or pupa body is the most important thing to imitate in the artificial. And hooks should be fine and thin themselves, to keep the imitation floating high in the water column. I use the sighted-nymph technique and the slightly-sunken technique mostly when fishing midge hatches and pre-hatches. But, at times, a small midge pattern on 8x, with a size 8 split shot about 14 inches up from the fly, can be fished near the bottom with great success. I often use this at-the-bottom combination after a mayfly hatch has petered out but the hatching of midges is not yet apparent. Interestingly, I seem to catch as many fish with this on-the-bottom technique using a midge pupa imitation as I do with a midge larva imitation.

But when a midge hatch is in full swing, the way it often is during July in between the PMD and Sulphur hatches, I use the slightly sunken midge pupa technique far more than I use floating midge adults. Often, by this time of the day, I have already used the upstream slightly-sunken mayfly nymph technique quite a lot. I find, therefore, that I need to turn around and fish the water I have just traveled through – fishing and wading it downstream – in order to connect consistently with the midge pupa. Indeed, my choice of tactics is almost always determined by what I have been doing and what the other, competing fishermen have been doing in the water that is now vacant.

If the next piece of water I intend to fish has been vacated by others, I will have noted what techniques they were using. I should be able to figure out by simple observation whether they were fishing on the surface, slightly under the surface, or well under the surface. I may not be able to tell which flies they were using, but often I also hear this information given out during the shouts, laughter, or expletives that fly fishermen expel as they cover the water with one or more companions. And if, due to a particularly crowded day, the next piece of water I will fish is the section of creek through which I have just traversed, I'll plan on changing flies, tactics, and terminal gear, from those I had just used.

This is a very important point to keep in mind. In the spring creeks, the large populations of fish and the large amount of food for these fish, keeps them feeding more or less all day long. Especially during the summer months, the population of fishermen is also very high and those fishermen can be expected to be pretty darn sophisticated, especially the ones that you know are "regulars". *Therefore, an important tool in your kitbag should be for you to be continually aware of what those around you are using for terminal tackle.* Is the fisherman using an indicator that you can see from your vantage point perhaps 80 feet away? If so, it generally means that the fisherman is using a weighted nymph pattern, for if the fisherman were using a slightly-sunken nymph, the indicator would be much smaller and closer to the fly – you probably won't be able to see the indicator from your vantage point. If there is no indicator at all, the fisherman is probably fishing a dry fly – dun, spinner, emerger, or floating nymph. Do there seem to be rising fish around the fisherman? Is he doing a lot of false casting? If so, you can bet with great certainty that he's using a dry fly, since this is the preferred method for most visitors to the creeks, including the very few, very skilled fishermen that use the dry fly not because they are novices at nymph fishing, but because they truly prefer the dry, seeing the fly drift without drag, seeing the trout open its mouth to inhale the fly. If that is what's going on upstream of you, you can be assured that your catch rate will be enhanced if you fish a nymph through their water, as soon as they vacate the place. Further, it will be highly likely that this "mismatching the fisherman hatch" will work no matter the time of day or the stage of activity of the relevant insects.

This mismatching of the fisherman's hatch works both ways. That is, although I tend to fish the nymph or pupa more than the dry, I often find myself in a situation that, given the behavior of those that came before me, suggests I have to concentrate on using the dry. Many times the angler vacating the spot I'm now entering was fishing a nymph. So I'll start using a dry immediately upon entering the vacated water.

If the fisherman before me is truly skilled, he will be changing terminal tackle and tactics frequently, just as I do. If I see him getting lots of hookups, while continually changing tactics, then I'm pretty sure I'll have trouble fishing his water when he vacates the spot. There is no simple "he was using dries, so I'll use nymphs" conclusion. When I do enter his vacated section, I'll concentrate on using the tactics and terminal tackle that are at the extremes of my "probability distribution."

The concept of a probability distribution needs explaining. Put aside the behavior of the fishermen for a moment and think about what an individual trout must be facing as he looks upstream for his next meal. During any moment on any given day, this flow of *real* food has a probability distribution associated with it. During late June-early July, we know that there will be a PMD pre-hatch and hatch period, followed by a midge hatch, followed by a Sulphur pre-hatch and hatch period. We also know that the exact timing of these activities is uncertain, and that a particular activity might occur earlier or later than we expect, and some activities may overlap other activities (2 or 3 insect-types being seen during the same time period). This means that at any given moment, there might be any of several types of food drifting down to our hungry trout.

Let's assume for the moment that the trout in question is elevated – he's high in the water column. During this particular time of this particular day, the probability of any particular insect-form drifting into the trout's window has a value associated with it. Suppose we are talking about being in one of the large pools at Armstrong's on July 1 at precisely 11 A.M. From experience we know that it is highly likely that this will be the middle of an actual PMD hatch, which might last another 2 hours. Let's assign this activity a probability of, say, 20% -- by this we mean that there's a 20% chance that the next insect to come into the trout's field of view is an actual Pale Morning dun. At this precise moment, however, it is also possible that the trout may next see a Pale Morning spinner float by – a remainder from the hatch of the previous day. Let's say this probability is only 1%. Now let's keep going. Even if we are really in the middle of the hatch, we know that the next piece of food coming by could be a slightly submerged PMD nymph (a real one).

Furthermore, we know that all PMD duns get to be duns by the nymph swimming to the surface and molting into a dun. We also know that not all nymphs are successful in escaping their shucks and becoming duns. Therefore, whatever is the probability of a floating dun being the next insect for the trout to see, the probability that it will be a slightly submerged nymph is higher, let's say 40%. Going further, we know that it is also possible that at this same instant, at exactly 11A.M., it is also possible that a Sulphur nymph or a midge pupa or even an "in-the-drift" midge larva can come drifting into view for this elevated trout. I am not aware of anyone actually having conducted a scientific study of these varying probabilities of what the trout might see next. But if such a study were to be conducted, the result would be something like the following diagram. The graphic is an invention, but it represents what might be called "expert judgment" based on absolutely no data except for long years of observation.

Probability Graph:
11A.M., July 1
Elevated fish

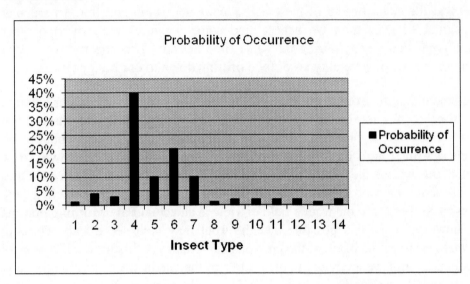

Insect Types:
1 = midge larva
2 = midge pupa
3 = midge adult
4 = PMD nymph
5 = PMD emerger
6 = PMD dun
7 = PMD crippled dun

8 = PMD spinner
9 = Sulphur nymph
10 = Sulphur emerger
11 = Sulphur dun
12 = Sulphur crippled dun
13 = Sulphur spinner
14 = All other – caddis, etc.

The probability graph separates the insect types into 14 arbitrary categories. The graph indicates that 4 stages of the PMD – nymph, emerger, dun, crippled dun -- are the most likely piece of food to come into the trout's view in the next moment, with the nymph being the highest probability. This high probability of a nymph drifting into the trout's view is due to some common-sense reasons.

First, as we've said, not all nymphs make their way to the surface to emerge as duns. Many get eaten by trout, some fail to push through the meniscus and therefore get eaten by trout further downstream, and some might drift until they get caught in some flotsam near a bank or partially submerged log. So, there must always be more nymphs in the water than there are duns on the surface. Most importantly, we know that the fisherman fishing the slightly sunken nymph will do better than the equally skilled fisherman fishing the dun imitation. My own observations say that the slightly sunken nymph will out-fish the dun <u>at least</u> 2 to 1 – that's why I put 40% as the probability of the fish seeing a nymph next as opposed to a 20% chance of his seeing a dun next. But remember, no one, so far as I know, has done a real probability study of this nature. I really have no idea of these *absolute* probabilities – it would take some doing just to figure out how to catch 100% of all the insects that are flowing past a given square foot of surface (and within, say, 12 inches underneath that particular piece of surface) during a particular period of time. Then, you'd have to identify and count properly all these insects caught in your net, all squished into a big mess. I'm working on it.

But the graph is probably not too far off with regard to the *relative* probabilities of each insect type appearing in the trout's view. This means that for each fish in your immediate vicinity (either fish that you can see or expect to be there – and are within easy casting distance without drag), you should go through the Big 4 probabilities (PMD nymph, PMD emerger/floating nymph, PMD dun, PMD crippled dun) before you consider some other artificial – if we are talking about an elevated fish at 11 A.M. on July 1 on Armstrong's. But suppose we are talking about 2P.M. on that same day, same pool, same creek. Then, you are likely to be in a pre-hatch or hatch period for midges – midge pupae and midge adults may have a higher probability of occurring then than any of the Big 4 PMD insect-types. Later in that same day, July 1, the odds are high that you'll have a Sulphur pre-hatch and hatch (although a less dense hatch than at the end of July). So, at, say 4P.M. on that day, when you see some evidence that elevated fish are actively feeding again, your highest probabilities should be associated with the Big 4 Sulphur types rather than the Big 4 PMD types.

Now, think about combining what you know about the relative probabilities of insect-types, with the reality of having to move into water that has just been vacated by another fisherman. On this same July 1, suppose that you have ardently and thoroughly fished 100 feet of a big pool and that you see a fisherman exit right upstream of you. Especially if you know the piece of water he has vacated to be a good piece (easier conditions in terms of drag-free floats), you immediately move upstream to claim it as your own. But instead of it being 11A.M., it is now 1:30P.M. Also, you have seen that the evacuated fisherman had been false-casting almost all the time and appeared never to use an indicator, even a small one. OK. Now, the combination of the time-of-day, coupled with your observations of what the last fisherman has been doing, point you to two good choices for terminal tackle. First, the PMD hatch might not be completely over and those fish now in front of you may not have seen an artificial PMD nymph today. Second, if the PMD hatch really is over, then those always-hungry-but-arrogant-rainbows might easily fall for a slightly sunken midge pupa imitation – because that is the next hatch due up any time now.

By trying both of these sub-surface patterns you might easily be catching fish in a part of the creek just vacated by a fisherman who has already been highly successful. You've combined your knowledge of the hatches with your keen observations of what your competition was doing. Cool. But suppose that after several minutes of accurate, drag free casting, you have not had a strike. Now is the time to think – "I need to move further down on the probability list of insect types." So, what has a lower probability of occurring than PMD/midge/sulphur types, but still higher probability than a caddis hatch on July 1 at 1:30P.M.?" Ah. Welcome to the world of scuds and sow-bugs.

11. Scuds and Sow-bugs.

The episode that day on the Itchen taught me about sight-fishing and about the scud. Today, on the spring creeks of Paradise, I do a lot of sight-nymphing, but it is done mainly with PMD and Sulphur nymphs and with midge larvae and pupae. The scud is reserved for those times when mayflies and midges are doing little to attract a crowd of feeding fish. This is probably a mistake on my part, because scud make up a very large proportion of the protein available to the trout, especially in the weedier sections of the creeks.

The scud, order Amphipoda, usually genus Gammarus, shouldn't be confused with true fresh-water shrimp, order Decapoda. So far as I know there are no significant populations of the latter in the Livingston spring creeks. But scuds are plentiful. Borger, in his book <u>Naturals</u>, quotes Pennak (1953) that scuds may number tens of thousands in a square meter of weed bed. I have not come close to seining this many scuds in the Montana spring creeks. Nevertheless, the essential point to take away is that scuds do indeed provide for quite a lot of trout food. Perhaps several dozen or even several hundred per cubic foot of weed is possible -- and if the weed bed is deep, it is possible that Pennak's anecdotal number is appropriate.

One thing we did do, with attention to detail, is raise scuds in one of our aquariums in the basement of our old house in Paradise Valley – a house located in the aptly named Spring Creek Hills sub-division. We started out by raising mayfly nymphs, and during the first few days of this exercise (sometime in the late 1970's) we learned that you have to place netting over the top of the aquarium, or you're likely to return home from a hard day's fishing to find the entire basement filled up with flying duns, or even mating spinners. The netting also solved the problem of being able to easily capture the duns and spinners in order to take macro-photographs of the creatures. Interestingly, you can pick up a mayfly dun or spinner with a pair of flat specimen tweezers, then place them on a small stick mounted in a fly-tying vise.[28] If the stick is placed mostly vertically, up into the air, wherever you place the mayfly it will crawl up

---

[28] Some such tweezers are made specifically for capturing fragile specimens such as mayflies. They consist of a very light, very flexible metal. I had misplaced ours recently and found that the tweezers, and almost anything else you need for entomological work, can be found at BioQuip Products, Inc., www.bioquip.com.

to the highest point of the stick and stay right there for many long minutes while you conduct your photography. Try that with caddis and it doesn't work – they fly off in an instant, after walking crazily all over the mounting stick. However, you can place a jar of adult caddis in the refrigerator for awhile, to calm them down before placing them on your vise-held stick.

It wasn't until several years of working with the nymphs that it occurred to us to start raising scuds. We wanted to know how they behave in the water. Importantly, we learned that scuds are fairly strong swimmers. These suckers can move – maybe not like Baetis, but pretty darn well. However, their swimming movements occur in short spurts, followed by a few seconds of inactivity, floating at whatever depth they were previously swimming. Also important is the observation that the scud appears to be stretched out lengthwise while swimming, but, in its "resting" time, it is curled up. This curled-up attitude is what is imitated by most scud flies you see on the market. And most of us use such curled-up imitations, because there is some logic to this. Why should the trout expend energy chasing the stretched-out swimming scud, when, instead the fish can simply wait for the drifting-curled-up phase – an easier target -- that will surely occur within a very short period of time? Another reason why almost all scud imitations are tied on curled hooks is that whenever we capture scud in our seining nets on the stream, we see them in a curled position in the net. You'd probably curl up in a fetal position too if some mammoth creature suddenly scooped you up in its net and raised you up out of your natural H_2O environment. Anyway, someday we'll have to conduct an experiment on straight-bodied scud imitations versus curled-bodied ones. In the meantime, keep using the curled body ones you can readily find in fly-shops.

As you will see in the chapter on tying, there are two major types of scud imitation – Al Troth's famous plastic-bag tie, and a newer generation of "sparkle scud." These two categories are sufficiently different (and must look different to the fish) that it's advisable to keep both kinds in your fly box. Size and color are also important – my own box contains scud from size 14 down to size 18, in both gray and olive colors (I'm referring to the color of the dubbing that imitates their body and legs.) Pink scud are highly useful other places, such as on the Missouri or the Big Horn, but I have not seined pink scud in the spring creeks and have not found that switching to a pink scud helps. Nor have I found it important to imitate the egg-sac on a scud by putting in a red-colored bit of dubbing at the rear of the crustacean. On the other hand, I fish a scud imitation for perhaps no more than an hour each day – there being all kinds of other food types to interest the trout throughout the rest of the day. So, I'd be pleased to hear from anyone who finds that pink scuds or egg-sac scuds are important in their arsenal for the Livingston creeks.

Let's talk now about that hour or so when you will indeed be using a scud on one of the spring creeks. You will be led to use a scud by a process of elimination. There won't be very many risers or elevated fish, perhaps none at all that you can see. You will probably be in a "between-hatches" period of the day. And/or you may be entering water that previously was thoroughly fished by a skilled angler using surface or near-surface methods. Or, you may be induced to use the scud by seeing a very specific clue – that of a clearly visible trout banging its head into the weeds, then backing away and opening its mouth to catch whatever its head-banging has dislodged from those weeds. Most of us have seen this kind of behavior and know that it might not be scud the trout is after. Baetis nymphs, for example, often reside in weed beds, in contrast to Ephemerella nymphs that often reside in gravel. But in the food-rich environment of the spring creeks, I can't say I've ever seen a trout doing its head-banging routine during a mayfly pre-hatch or hatch period. It just isn't an efficient use of his energy. The head-banging will occur mainly during the "dry periods" of the day, when the dry-fly purist usually is sitting on the bank waiting for the next hatch period to begin.

It is during these dry spells that you can have a blast with scuds. Besides, a true spring creek enthusiast would never actually take a real lunch break, right? Begin your "scudding" by first looking for a feeding trout that is in fairly shallow water. This fish will allow you to use a sighted nymph technique (actually a sighted-scud technique) without having to use any weight on the scud imitation or on the tippet. Because scud are never taken extremely high in the water column, the use of a heavy-wire hook is all that you'll need to get the fly down near the bottom to a fish feeding in maybe 18" of water. Some experimenting will help you figure out how far upstream of the trout to pitch the scud, but here again it helps to use a very light tippet. An 8x tippet, if you've learned how to handle it with a 2-weight rod, can be important to your success, but 7x will suffice in many circumstances. Again, do not make the mistake of thinking that sub-surface fishing permits the use of heavier tippets than in dry fly fishing. It's just the opposite – the trout can see more clearly under the surface than through the distorting effect of the surface film. And any imitation – scud or nymph or pupa – bounces around more freely when attached to a lighter weight tippet.

My best fish ever on the spring creeks was a 23.5 inch brownie (yes, a dumb brownie) taken in 12 inches of water on Nelson's with 8x and an un-weighted Troth scud. After the hook-up we went back and forth under a log many times before the steady, always steady, pressure brought him to the net. And as I indicated earlier, Suzanne's best fish ever was also taken on 8x, on Armstrong's, with a size 18 olive pheasant-tail. It was a 24.5 inch rainbow (very smart, but too cocky) whose landing was a delight to observe in the big pool by the parking lot. The spring creek fly shops are now beginning to stock the new breed of 8x tippets, such as G-Max FX. At $15 per spool this stuff is not cheap,[29] but the quality of your tippet, the size of your line, and the quality and shape of your fly, are what really matters out here – that and extremely accurate casting in the wind.

The actual mechanics of sight-fishing the scud have been discussed already in the chapter on sight-fishing the nymph. One difference, however, is that a size 16 scud can sometimes actually be seen in the water, when fishing to a trout in shallow water with the sun at your back. That is, a size 16 scud, with its large sparkle fibers, is a whole lot bigger than a size 18 skinny Baetis nymph. Remember, extremely accurate casting is what's needed in sight fishing, and this is especially true of a trout in shallow water – a trout that will be somewhat more spooky than the average trout. You have to learn, by trial and error, how close you can get to such a fish, because close proximity is a key to success in placing the fly exactly the 6 inches from the weeds that the trout is holding, and exactly the 2 or 3 feet upstream of the trout needed to drift the imitation into its mouth. So get close, but not too close. Sometimes you can get to within 12

---

[29] Other great brands of 8x include Power-Full, Frog's Hair, Orvis SuperStrong and Rio Powerflex. Still others I haven't yet given a good workout. Note that none of the 8x tippets measure a true 0.003 inches in diameter. Using a good micrometer, I got the following readings for these particular brands: G-Max FX at .00385, Orvis SS at 0.0037, Frog's Hair and Power-Full at 0.0036, and Rio Powerflex at 0.0034. Climax Fluorocarbon 8x is 0.0043, significantly thicker than a true 7x. The G-Max is the strongest of the 8x tippets we've tried, and the Rio the weakest. Note also that no 7x among these brands is exactly 0.004 inches in diameter either. Among the 7x tippets, G-Max and Power-Full are 0.0045, Orvis SS is 0.0044, and Rio is 0.0041. Climax 7x Fluorocarbon mikes out at 0.0055, which is thicker than a true 6x! Note also that tippet diameter changes across manufacturing lots and even across different strands of the same spool. I use Frog's Hair 8x when a particular fish is very tippet shy; I use the G-Max FX 8x for most of my fishing because of its suppleness and strength; and I rarely use the Rio 8x because it does not have the stretching capability and breaks somewhat more easily than the others. Power-Full is extremely difficult to obtain in the U.S., and you should watch out for spools that are several years old on a fly shop's shelf.

or 15 feet of a trout feeding in shallow water on the far side of some faster moving water. Seeing the strike in such shallow water will generally not be a problem, except if the strike is to a real insect, not your imitation. Since you generally *won't* be able to see your fly, make sure that your strike is violent enough to move the hook into the trout's mouth if that is where your fly really is, but not so violent that the act of striking (while the trout is eating a real insect, not your artificial) puts the trout down.

Sight-fishing the scud is like sight-fishing the nymph in that most of your fishing will be at *right-angles* to the trout, not casting directly upstream or downstream. When fishing a slightly sunken nymph during the height of the hatch it is quite possible to cast directly upstream to an elevated fish so long as you don't put too much of the tippet over the trout. But when you are fishing the scud it will generally be <u>after</u> you've had all that fun with mayfly imitations to bulging fish and true risers. The scudding fish in shallow water generally will be somewhat warier than the elevated fish during a frenetic hatch. He will have learned to be wary of tippet material. You don't want to place too much of the tippet or any of the leader over the fish. This means fishing at right angles or maybe even casting slightly across and downstream. Remember, depending on where the sun is in relation to your fish, even 8x tippet (the portion that is not sunk to the level of the fish) can cast a moving shadow on the bottom. Keep your casts slightly to the near side of the sighted fish, if possible.

Your attempt not to line a fish at right angles to you sometimes gets you into trouble. Suzanne and I fished every summer on the Beaverhead with Al Troth, the internationally known fly tyer and guide. Back then, Al tied just about all of our flies, and we had a big portion of our budget each year go to these exquisite olive pheasant tails and to the emerging midge patterns that, after all these years, still are not duplicated by other tyers. It was Al who taught us the importance of long tippets – no one we see fishing anywhere today would even guess that we typically use tippets of 5 feet or even longer. One day on the Beaverhead we were at a right-angle pool on a side channel. I just couldn't get the couple of risers to take the dry, because I got drag right before the fly entered the strike zone. After a whole bunch of casts, I said "How about another fly?" Al said, "Give me your line." I did, and he tied on a 6 foot tippet, then tied on the same dry fly. You guessed it – first cast with the new rig and I was into a fish.

It was also Al who taught me an important lesson about sight-fishing the scud. We had launched his boat at the most upstream end of the tail-water, just about within sight of the Canyon Ferry dam. Before floating, however, Al saw some fish upstream of the boat, on the far side of the river, near some weed beds. He and I waded out into the current while Suzanne readied her camera. We got within easy casting distance of a couple of nice fish that I could see moving right and left in the current very close to the bottom. We put on a Troth scud and about a size 4 split shot to get down to them and I began to cast. After several casts, I stopped and said "What am I doing wrong?" Al said, "You're not covering the closest fish, your casts are missing him by several feet to our side." This couldn't be, I thought -- it was late in the season and I was well practiced, doing quite well on the spring creeks. Nevertheless, I made several casts a couple of feet further out. Al said, "You're not correcting for light refraction. Try to cast well beyond the fish and we'll see which way it turns to take the fly." Sure enough, I made the next cast to a spot that appeared to be about 6 feet or so beyond the fish, and the fish turned a few inches *toward* us and ate something. Al said "set" and I did, and the fish was gone down the current, requiring us to move way downstream to net him. That happened over 25 years ago, and I think about it every time I sight fish with a scud. *The deeper the water, the more likely you'll need to correct quite a bit for light refraction*[30]

Now suppose you've exhausted your tries on all the visible fish in shallow water. You'll now need to think about fishing the scud blind into deeper water. Many times, I wind up casting a weighted scud into 3 or 4 feet of water, in the same region of the stream that I just had a blast casting to elevated fish during the hatch. But now I can't see any fish, so I'm fishing blind with a #8 split shot clamped about 12 or 14 inches up from the scud (on my 8x tippet). The casting and fishing technique is exactly as described in the chapter on fishing the weighted nymph blind – the "right angle" technique. In this fishing it is important to be sensitive to getting the

---

[30] I'm not a scientist, so I can't confirm that refraction *per se* is behind my failure to cast far enough to reach the trout holding deep in the water. It is also possible that I am falling victim to a simple illusion. When I see a trout rising or holding a couple of inches under the surface I instinctively pick some reference point on the surface to adjust my cast (perhaps I am looking at some protruding weeds and the riser is one foot closer to me than those exposed weeds). Now, when the same trout is holding in the same place relative to the surface, but at a depth of 4 feet, I notice that I must lower by head (lower my eyes) to look at the trout. To me, it now appears closer to me because, instinctively, I would be looking almost straight down at a trout holding at my feet. So I therefore conclude that I must cast to a spot on the surface of the water that is closer to me than the one foot from the exposed weed the rising trout was located. In relation to something on the surface of the water, I cast closer to my position, even though the trout is holding right under the same spot on the surface of the water.

scud down very near the bottom. You will have been spending several wonderful hours without even remembering that you have a box of split shot with you, and it's easy to make the mistakes of a) having too light a split shot, or b) too small a distance between the hook and the strike indicator. In this kind of fishing, I often find that the trout feels so safe on the bottom, after all the hours of hectic activity near the surface, that the takes are pretty decisive.

Often, when the fly is in the imagined "strike zone", and the indicator and rod tip are slightly downstream of you, the indicator won't just hesitate – it will move sharply toward where the fish is, and you will have "auto-hooked" a trout. Remember, there was still plenty of skill involved in choosing the right spot, the right fly, the right weight, and the right distance to the strike indicator, so don't feel like this type of sport is beneath you. And you will be playing a nice trout, while the dry fly purist is sitting on the bench with his afternoon bottle of Chablis, thinking "ugh, I wouldn't stoop to such shenanigans." Until about the 3rd or 4th fish in a row that you hook and release – then, invariably, the age-old question is asked, "What are you using?" No, you may not say "worms." The code of the spring-creek-nympher is always to say exactly what you are using, down to the size of the fly and the size of the tippet. This will be so unbelievable that it will have the same effect as telling a bald-faced lie. Either way, the information will not register, will not be remembered.

I've waited until the end of this chapter to introduce the sow-bug. In my past observations, sow-bugs had been less prevalent than scud in the Livingston spring creeks. And they seemed to be somewhat more prevalent on DePuy's than upstream in Armstrong's. These observations have not been confirmed by the kind of scientific sampling that Dan Gustafson does in his quest to catalogue the mayflies of Montana, so don't read too much into it. The simple fact is that it helps to have some sow-bug imitations in your box because it just might be the case that a particular fish may have a preference for such a pattern. Or, much more likely, after screwing up a particular fish with your scud imitation, you might try a couple of other fish, then come back to the first fish using a sow-bug instead of a scud. As a general rule, never cover a fish, even after some long minutes, with the same fly he has just rejected, or worse, has bitten and you missed the strike. As we've said before, it is as important to know when to truly rest a particular fish as it is to choose the right terminal tackle.

As the season wears on, and my skills return to their mid-season level, I become very good at

NOT fishing. Mostly, I make no more than 3 or so casts to any fish, before switching fish or tactics or both. This is never more important than when sight-fishing or blind-fishing the scud. So have those sow-bug imitations just in case and, in the chapter on fly imitations, you'll see that it's hard to beat Lee Kinsey's sow-bug recipe. You should also know that we are beginning to suspect that sow-bug populations, relative to scud populations, have changed. Last year, toward the end of October we did some seining on the big pool by the parking lot on Armstrong's. We were astounded to see that we captured many sow-bugs, including some in the size 14 range, but very few scud. This year, in early June, we repeated our seining in DePuy's and Armstrong, and the population of sow bugs relative to scud was even higher than last fall. Since we haven't seined for over a decade, since before the floods of the late 1990's, it may be that this represents an important population shift – or not. In any case, don't go to the streams without at least a few of Lee's size 16-18 sow bugs. You can find these at Buzz Basini's shop at the upper end of DePuy's. You get to the shop by turning into the Armstrong Spring Creek road (at the sign with the red arrow), then at the first bend in the road turn left and down to Depuy's rather than right and on to the O'Hair's house.

A couple of more things you should know about sow-bugs is that, first, there appears to be something of a difference in color between what we call "sow-bugs" on the Montana spring creeks and what the Eastern fly fishers call "cress bugs". Most fly fishers have viewed sow-bugs and cress bugs as being different names for the same creature (see Heck, p.85). And it is true that the east coast and mountain west versions are indeed both Isopoda. However, our spring creek sow-bugs have very little greenish color, and look brownish on the back, with the clearly prominent dark strip down the back, with light tan colored legs. There is very little green color in our sow-bugs compared to cress-bugs.

Also, the sow-bug differs from the scud in that the sow-bug's "legs" are very fine and fairly narrow compared to the scud. The scud uses those large legs to swim quite rapidly, while the sow-bug generally crawls quickly. For example, when placed in a small jar of water, the scud will be swimming fast laps in circles, while the sow-bug will go to the bottom and crawl quickly along on the bottom. The sow-bug and scud, viewed from the top don't look dramatically different from each other. But, when viewed from the side, a live and active sow bug is fairly thin compared to a scud. Still, at rest or curled up in alarm, both insects look something like a very small shrimp. So it is quite possible that trout often mistake one for the other. Nevertheless, I highly recommend using two separate imitations. Below are macro photos taken recently of the two bugs. The photo of the sow bug is somewhat more magnified than the photo of the scud. Both photos show the insect in the water with some art paper as a background.

Scud, about a size 14.

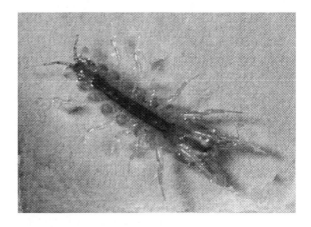

Sow-bug, about a size 16.

12. The Dry Fly.

OK, you are asking "what's a chapter on dry fly fishing got to do with a book on nymphing the spring creeks?" Well, this is a book about *learning* how to fish the spring creeks. The learning never stops. Yes, it is true that I often spend an entire day without making a single cast using a floating imitation. But there are many other days that involve perhaps 25-30% of my hook-ups using floating flies – when the various nymphing tactics are not working extremely well. Let's start off with how to determine that dry fly fishing is your best bet.

First, as in other instances discussed earlier, it always pays to think about switching tactics with regard to a single fish. Indeed, thinking about an individual sighted fish should be your objective through-out the day, unless conditions and fish-activity strongly suggest blind fishing the nymph. I try *never* to blind fish the dry, except with a couple of casts to another likely spot, immediately after screwing up on a particular rising fish. This self-imposed no-blind-fishing rule arises partly out of a sense of best-practice, and partly out of a code of ethics. If fish in general can't be seen because they aren't elevated and/or are not rising (at least with bulging rises), then I feel it is wrong to blind fish the dry. That's right -- this is the opposite of the dry-fly fisherman's purist view that blind-fishing the dry is somehow ethically superior to blind-fishing the nymph (or even sight-fishing the nymph). I feel this way because, when *truly* blind-fishing the dry on the advanced trout of the spring creeks, you will only catch a few fish (those at the "tail" of the probability distribution), and they will tend to be brownies.

What I mean by "truly blind-fishing the dry" is that you are casting a dry fly during a time of the day or year when there are virtually no visible elevated fish and no rises (including bulging rises). This means that the huge bulk of the fish population is concentrating on other kinds of food well below the surface, not just immediately below the surface. If you convince a single trout to rise through several feet of water to take a dry, it means either that there isn't much food below the surface available to the trout (highly unlikely on any day of the year, even the winter, on the spring creeks), or that this particular trout will take anything. Blind-fishing the dry to such an unseen trout is beneath my dignity, or what's left of it in my old age.

On the freestones, the individual trout that "will take anything" is not rare (think of blind fishing the dry on Rock Creek, near Missoula). On a particular day or time of day, food is sufficiently scarce (not available to the trout, even though the mayfly nymphs or caddis larvae are somewhere, hidden) that many trout will rise through 4 or more feet of water to take something that looks roughly real on the surface. I do not object to this kind of blind dry fly fishing and have done it many times. On the spring creeks, however, I think that blind-fishing the dry during the inter-hatch periods or during the pre-hatch period represents a weak spot in the angler's skills.

Further, some anglers with poor eyesight (me, now in my old age), or with limited experience, will *think* they are blind-fishing a dry, because the angler cannot see several fish that are elevated. An elevated fish may concentrate on taking sub-surface nymphs, but the elevated fish may also take a few floating nymphs, emergers, and duns. So, fishing a dry over an elevated fish that does not often rise is perfectly acceptable in my weird code of ethics, even desirable, as we shall see below. However, many times I have watched a dry-fly fisherman cast over several trout that are not only elevated but occasionally making true rises (taking floating nymphs, duns, whatever) or bulging rises. If the rises are difficult for me to see, it is likely that they are difficult for the other fisherman to see. The angler will give no indication that he sees these fish, often fishing elsewhere in a 360 degree arc, in a methodical manner. When the dry is cast over the unseen fish, the angler reacts with surprise if the trout takes the fly. I imagine that, later, he says to his friends that he did OK "blind fishing" the comparadun, or whatever is his dry fly of choice. In my own view of the world, however, that angler was not blind-fishing the dry – he was simply blind-fishing the fish.

To me, dry fly fishing is required in several circumstances: a) when a particular trout, or a group of trout, indicate a clear preference for a surface imitation, b) when you have tried a slightly submerged tactic on a particular elevated fish or group of elevated fish without success, c) when you have moved into a position which has recently been vacated by a skilled sub-surface fisherman who probably has NOT used a surface imitation, or d) when surface glare will not permit you to sight fish the nymph and, as well, there is evidence that the trout are shy of the micro-indicator. Also, as the season goes on, I find that many fish of the spring creek have been educated by my own nymph tactics and my own particular nymph imitations. As August comes and goes, I find that fishing a surface imitation often does better (for me) than fishing a sub-surface imitation to a particular group of trout, several of which I have already released a few times during the season.

If we are talking about the early to middle portion of the season (prior to mid-August), there will be times during the day when you can see a particular fish taking a smorgasbord of food – surface flies and subsurface flies alike. Sometimes you make your first cast to such a fish using a slightly sunken nymph. Then you change to another sub-surface slightly sunken pattern. If these 2 perfect casts fail to get a response, and if you see the fish continue to occasionally rise, your chance of a hook-up might be higher with a surface imitation.

There is one condition, however, that must be met for you to successfully use a dry fly on the tough trout of the spring creeks. The trout –whether a free-riser or an occasionally-rising, sub-surface/on-surface "variable feeder" trout -- must be *across and/or downstream* from you, never upstream of you. The exception is when the water is sufficiently choppy to hide your tippet. That is, your chances of success with a surface imitation are always highest when insuring that the fly reaches the fish before the tippet does. Take a look at the successful dry fly fishermen on the spring creeks. They always seem to be casting downstream with a "stop cast", causing the tippet to bounce backward toward the caster in order to create S-curves in the transition and tippet sections of the leader.

I like to tell a story about one of the very best, if not the best, dry-fly fishermen on the creeks, Buzz Basini, who owns the Spring Creek Specialists fly shop on DePuy's. One day in the fall, I was fishing the PhD pool when Buzz drove over the culvert to his shop. I was preparing to move upstream to the curve above the PhD pool (which, I thought, I better get to right away or Buzz might beat me there). After getting a few fish on the sunken nymph at and above the curve, I saw Buzz walking along the bank toward me, geared up. He asked if he could go into the creek immediately below me. He knew I was nymphing upstream, and he would cast the dry fly downstream, through water I had just fished. We fished for awhile almost back to back and Buzz took a couple of fish right away in this "just fished" water. He then came up on the bank opposite me to take a rest and chat. After a while, the upstream nymphing turned slow and I happened to look downstream and saw a fish rising right up against the weeds on the far bank. I asked Buzz if I could borrow his rod with his dry, then I waded over to hand him my rod (with a weighted PT) and get his rod in exchange. One Winston rod exchanged for another.

Naturally, my cast to the riser was not exactly perfect, and I put the fish down. Then, when I turned back to Buzz, I saw him holding his cell phone next to my rod. It took a few seconds for it to sink in – Buzz Basini was using his cell phone to take a digital photograph of my super-secret Lee Kinsey nymph secured in the hook-holder of my rod!! He claimed that he wanted to get a photo to see if someone would tie the fly for his shop – but probably he wanted to black-mail Lee into tying some of the nymphs for Buzz's own collection. You will see this nymph in the next chapter, because the word is now out (but I was planning on writing this all down anyway).

So, let's say that conditions are optimal for using a dry. Which one? How? The next chapter will give you a feel for which ones. The chapter on Game Plan includes a discussion on casting and terminal tackle, but will not deal with casting technique very much – at least with respect to dry fly fishing -- because you won't be reading this book and planning to fish the Paradise spring creeks if you are an unpracticed neophyte. But here are some major points. First, I find that, with so many good dry fly fishermen on the creeks, using "ordinary" dry flies is not very productive. And remember, you will be using the dry fly during very specific times of the day, when everyone will be casting some sort of comparadun or thorax fly, and an individual fish is clearly rising. Sure, these "normal" flies should be in your box and, sure, we would probably not have known about these flies without the path-breaking work of Swisher and Richards, Caucci and Nastasi, and Vince Marinaro.

But when the time of day comes that you feel you should switch to the dry, and you turn to face downstream to execute your plan, you should think about a few things that will set your flies apart from the others. First, the fly should ride low in the water. Second, the fly body should be sufficiently skinny to match the real thing. This is especially critical for the Baetis genus, but even on the PMDs I see fishermen using dry flies that are way too thick. Third, the body of your surface imitation should include some form of segmentation. I believe that segmentation is critical to surface fishing (as it is to nymph or pupa fishing) – it represents one of the triggers that screams "real thing" to the rising trout. For this purpose a quill body is wonderful. [31] So, using these 3 keys, let's go through the types of dry flies that we use.

---

[31] A.K. Best says it best – excuse the pun – "A single quill is the closest thing to a perfect representation of the spinner body I've discovered….Since the quill is about 90 percent air, trapped in thousands of tiny cells contained in the natural, enamel-like shell, its floating qualities are astoundingly good."

The floating nymph. I wrote my first article about the use of floating nymphs in the July/September 1980 issue of *Fly Fisherman*.[32] Of course, Skues introduced the concept and I think others have written about it as well, so it seems that there really is not much that's new in fly fishing. Back then, in the 1980's, my ties for the floating nymph were crude, the tippets were 4x, and we used Turle knots instead of Orvis knots to tie the fly onto the tippet. The fly line was a 5 weight, the leader/tippet combination was 9 feet long, and the strike indicator (when sub-surface fishing) was the end of the fly line. But I don't miss the good old days, only my better eyes and hand-eye coordination. Today, we use 2-weights with 13 foot to 16 foot leader/tippet combinations. Today, the flies are very delicately tied specifically for floating-nymph use (not simply the same nymph used for sub-surface fishing except without the split-shot and with a dab of dry-fly floatant). And today the tippet is 8x – with a diameter that is less than one-half that used in the early 1980's!!

But, 30 years later, the conditions are the same – highly elevated fish that are bulging and true-rising. Generally, the switch from the slightly-sunken nymph will occur after that particular technique loses its effectiveness. Still, it really helps to determine that some substantial portion of the trout population is truly rising. The only way to know for sure that the trout is rising to the dry, not bulging, is to look downstream and see the white of the trout's mouth as it opens and closes on the surface. If you can't clearly see that white mouth on at least one or two fish, then the fish are not truly rising, and it would be better to switch to a *downstream* slightly-sunken nymph technique rather than the upstream slightly-sunken technique. One more thing -- when you are in flat water and there is no wind to mask the sound, and no noise of other fishermen talking, you can often hear several rising fish make a sound when they open and close their mouths above the surface of the water. You can literally hear the "chomp" and it is a sweet sound indeed.

The floating nymph in construction and attitude differs from a true "emerger" pattern. The nymph represents the moments *before* the shuck splits and the dun begins to crawl out onto the

---

[32] Interestingly, I mentioned the slightly-sunken nymph as a great technique in that article, but it wasn't until micro-indicators were developed that this method became widespread. But, while the slightly-sunken nymph is used widely, it is NOT widely used with 8x, with extremely long tippets, with 2-weights, with properly proportioned nymph imitations, and with micro-mini-indicators. Good anglers know about the technique, but have not maximized their chances by using the entire *system* we have been describing.

surface. So, the floating nymph imitation should have a dark thorax area – it should look pretty much like the sunken nymph, except with a dry fly hook and treated with floatant.[33] The problem, of course, is -- how does the angler see such a low-riding dark fly on the surface, especially in a riffle? The answer, like always, is that the angler must be very accurate with the cast. If the angler doesn't see the fly hit the water, it will be very difficult for the eye to find the fly. This same issue is present when using the micro-indicator. But the floating nymph is even harder to see than a green or red micro-indicator. Moreover, you are most likely to be using the floating nymph *after* you have been using a micro-indicator (and a slightly sunken nymph) on a particular piece of water. So, your eyes have become used to picking up the micro-indicator and it will be difficult to adjust to the small black thorax area of the floating nymph – which is usually the part of the floating nymph that you see first. In flat water with glare, the black thorax area is sometimes quite easy to see, but in other conditions, especially in the chop of a riffle, the floating nymph will be very tough to see.

As a practical matter, casting accuracy solves everything. Accuracy, in turn, can most easily be accomplished by getting fairly close to the fish – just as you try to do in fishing the slightly-sunken nymph or in sight-nymphing. However, being highly accurate at short distances (20 feet and under) is something that most fly fishermen never practice. And, being highly accurate with a downstream "stop" cast (which is the same as Marinaro's "puddle" cast) – to create S-curves in the tippet – is extremely difficult with a long leader/tippet combination. Add into this mix the famous Paradise Valley winds and -- well, you get the picture. But if you *do* achieve accuracy, then oftentimes it won't matter if you can't see the floating nymph. You will know where the fly lands in relationship to the rising fish, and you will know when to strike as that fish rises to your unseen artificial.

Still, there are times and conditions when you don't have much of a clue where the floating nymph lands. In these conditions, there is no shame in using a micro-indicator. The trick in this circumstance is to a) make the micro-indicator very small (a *mini-micro-indicator*), b) attach the indicator about 30 inches or more up from the fly, and c) use the stop-cast. The reason for placing the indicator so far from the fly is that, when you stop the cast, the fly will bounce back

---

[33] It helps to have a turn of small hackle under the thorax area of the floating nymph, but this is not necessary. The hackle, clipped on top and bottom, acts to stabilize the nymph in the water and helps the angler to see the dark wing case. See the chapter on artificials.

toward the indicator as the rig lands on the water. You won't be able to see the fly but you know that it is about 12-20 inches from the indicator and down and across-stream from the indicator (remember, you are almost always fishing the dry fly down and across, or directly downstream). You watch this area near the indicator and you strike whenever any fish rises in this area. The key to the stop-cast is the same as in fishing any un-weighted fly on long, light tippets – high line speed. We'll spend more time on casting technique later.

This stop-cast then-watch technique is also necessary when you are using a truly tiny traditional dry fly – that is, a fly that, in its entirety, is the size of the wing case on a size 16 nymph pattern. One such fly that we use a lot is the Al Troth midge emerger pattern shown in the next chapter. Same thing goes for the Al Troth mayfly-emerger pattern. We started using these small dry flies in the early 1990's and they are dynamite during midge hatches and during the late summer sulphur hatches (when the Baetis duns seem even smaller, seem to sit even lower in the water, and the true risers are even more picky than in late July). Often, using the mini-micro-indicator will be the only way you will "see" a fly this small at a distance of 20 feet, especially in one of the riffles on Armstrong's in late August. At times I disguise the micro-indicator by using a permanent marking pen to color the indicator black. This is especially useful in glare conditions. Again, in the toughest situations, you don't use any indicator and you rely on your casting accuracy to tell you approximately where the fly should be. Any rise by any trout in this 2 foot square area is your signal to strike.

As we have discussed earlier, it is not necessary to use the very lightest tippet when fishing the dry fly as opposed to the nymph. So long as you are casting down and across, the fly should reach the trout before the tippet. That, coupled with the distorting effect of the meniscus, should allow you easily to use 7x for your dry fly fishing. Nevertheless, the lighter is the tippet the better are your chances when fishing either the dry fly or the nymph. With the new, more flexible and tougher 8x tippets on the market, I tend to use 8x straight through the day during late season, even when fishing the dry downstream.

However, an important issue when fishing downstream with the dry is – how do you strike, then play the fish? Since you are upstream of the fish, you don't have to worry too much about the direction in which you drive the rod-tip at the strike – there is usually no need to "strike to the bank" as when nymphing. However, downstream fishing eliminates any chance of "auto-hooking" – you simply do not have the benefit of the current driving the hook into the side of the trout's mouth. Moreover, when the trout rises to the dry fly, you must strike when the trout's mouth is closed, not earlier as it opens its mouth to inhale the fly, or later, when it opens its mouth a second time to reject the artificial. This requires the downstream dry fly strike to be a <u>tad slower</u> than the nymph strike. The latter takes place seemingly in a violent, quick as a flash manner, while the dry fly strike can be done in the more traditional, straight-up, leisurely fashion. One thing to remember, however, is that the infamous South Island rise from the large brown trout of New Zealand is definitely NOT the case in Paradise Valley. The South Island browns seem to hold their mouth open for a split second longer than you think they will, before they begin to chew on the fly (and they seem to chew longer than their American counterparts). So, the guides Down Under tell you to say "God Save the Queen" before you raise your rod tip to strike. The arrogant rainbows of the spring creeks, however, will often spit out the dry fly so fast that you will think you have received a rejection, not an honest-to-god strike. So your strike to the dry fly taken downstream of you should still be plenty quick.

The next tactical problem occurs the instant after you set the hook in the top of the mouth of the rising fish 20 feet downstream of you. Of course you must use a slip-strike – your left hand must be loosely holding the line so that the bolting fish will not be stopped by your inadvertent pinching of the line in your left hand (if you are a right-handed fisherman). But no matter what, no matter where, and no matter when, the just-hooked fish downstream of you is highly likely to turn and head further downstream, in a very great hurry. This is where the use of a high-quality click-drag reel becomes important. We have tried every known configuration of quality drag reel and we find that we lose too many fish while the line is trying to overcome the inertia of the drag. The click-drag reels seem to cut down on those lost fish.[34] And the lost fish are lost not so much by the 8x tippet breaking, but mainly from the hook pulling from the tip of the trout's mouth.

No matter which reel you use, however, you will find that down-stream dry fly fishing, just like down-stream nymphing, results in the hooked fish turning and running to a spot often well

---

[34] We use click-drag Abel™ reels now and, again, this is not a paid endorsement. Abel is still making the TR series, so far as we know, and we use the TR2 instead of the TR1, in order to have a larger spool diameter. Note that the click drag reels, any brand, are susceptible to dirt in the cogs of the gear that the click drag engages -- so clean these reels often.

down below you. Do not try to stop this initial run, it will only make the fish go further. Rather, keep very light pressure on the fly line with your left hand and wait for the fish to stop. Then, begin to exert pressure with your rod tip held to either side of the fish, causing the fish to pull against the line toward the opposite bank. Sometimes you can work the fish all the way upstream to the spot you are standing when the fish took the fly. Most times, however, especially with a fish over about 15" or so, you will need to wade down and toward the edge of the creek, in order to put enough side pressure on the fish to tire it. You don't want to wade down the center of the creek, because that will put down more risers than if you wade down the edge of the creek. Besides, the risers along the edge typically are those darn, dumb brownies. Just kidding.

Nevertheless, this is one of the big disadvantages of dry fly fishing. Since it is done mostly in a downstream fashion, it usually takes much longer to tire the fish and lead it to the net. Then, you have to wade back up along the bank to your spot before the strike. Then, you have to apply powdered desiccant to the fly to absorb the fish mucus, often followed by fly floatant, before you can resume your casting. What a bummer – dry fly fishing results in far fewer fish per hour than nymphing, because it takes so long to land each fish, and then resume casting! Oh well, somebody always has to do the dirty work or those spring creek rainbows would become unacceptably arrogant.

We should discuss at this point the "problem" mentioned by some people when we talk about fishing with 8x tippets. "You will take too long to fight the fish and this will kill some of the them – 8x is unsporting." Well, it would be if fished with a stiff rod and a 3 or 4 weight rod, as is mostly done by those few people who try it. The fact is that we play our fish on the spring creeks, with 8x, much, much faster than the average fisherman using 6x. With the light 2 weight and the flexible rod, we often have the rod bent *almost double* when landing the fish. And, as indicated earlier, the vast majority of lost fish on 8x involves the hook coming loose from the flesh on the inside of the mouth of the trout, just as it does with 6x.

Indeed, no matter where we fish, we try to come as close as possible to "horsing" the fish as we can. It is indeed not good for the fish to be played a long time. And, on the spring creeks, I try to horse even a fish that has gotten well downstream of me – even though this is likely to pull the hook out of its mouth. Only rarely, when the fish is very nice (over 18 inches in length), will I wade all the way down to the trout in order to land it.

The spinner. We use down-wing spinners a lot for surface fishing, but not because we fish a lot in the midst of a spinner fall. Ephemerella spinner falls often occur during daylight (early evening) in June or early July. But for the more prevalent Baetis genus, the spinner falls typically occur after dark. Perhaps this has to do with the tendency of these Baetis to swim below the surface to lay their eggs. That is, maybe the flies feel more vulnerable to being eaten by trout beneath the surface than if they lay their eggs while on the surface, so the sub-surface egg-layers wait until the cover of darkness.[35] Or, perhaps the after-dark egg-laying has to do with the air-temperature being too high during mid-summer daylight hours. In any event, the point is that spinner imitations can be very useful even when there are no spinners evident on the surface or in the air.

This effectiveness of spinners arises, we think, from the trout needing to see a surface imitation that differs in construction and attitude from all the comparadun and thorax flies being cast by other anglers. The properly tied spinner will have the same important 3 factors associated with constructing a floating nymph. It will be tied to float low in the surface film, it will be appropriately skinny, and it will have ribbing that is an important key to the trout. The properly tied spinner can be easily mistaken for a floating nymph. It can also be mistaken for a crippled dun. And, it can be taken for a true spinner, since, especially during the earlier season, the trout will have seen mornings when spinner falls are mixed in with hatching mayflies. So, the spinner pattern is a true jack-of-all-trades.

What is critical to tying the spinner is the use of only one or two wraps of hackle, clipped top and bottom to float the fly down in the film. Using a segmented body such as one made of stripped quill is also important. Small diameter gold wire can also be used for segmentation. Hen hackle-tip spinners and Zelon wing spinners are nowhere near as effective as clipped-

---

[35] See Hafele and Hughes, p. 47, in which the authors say that "some species" of Baetis lay their eggs under the surface, some on top. We don't know for sure that the Tricaudatus species fits this under-water label. We have certainly seen spent sulphurs on the surface of the spring creeks, but we haven't seen much in the way of before-dark transitions from mating flight to surface down-wings. Either way, the point is that while down-wing sulphur imitations on the surface can be quite useful, it is *not* because you will see a lot of Baetis egg-laying flights which result in lots of down-wing flies on the surface during daylight.

hackle spinners – spinners made with wound hackle that is clipped top and bottom. I think this is because the trout is easily put off by the massiveness of the Zelon winged or hackle-tip spinners compared with the real deal. Of course, like any fishing situation on the heavily-fished spring creeks, a particular trout may just have seen some artificial clipped-hackle spinner and may be much more interested in taking a large-density-wing pattern instead of the clipped-hackle pattern. So, it can never hurt to carry all 3 types of spinner patterns in your fly box – hen hackle, Zelon-winged, and clipped-hackle.

I often use the spinner pattern when I enter riffle water just vacated by another angler. Often, the angler will be using a Comparadun or thorax pattern with wings that stand high. The angler will even be fishing downstream. Indeed, many anglers now know that duns are to be fished in the riffles and nymphs/pupae are to be fished in the slow pools – just the opposite of old-fashioned reasoning. But when the angler stops seeing rises in the middle of the riffle, he may exit his position without realizing that it was his use of the high-and-dry imitation that caused the fish to stop true-rising. When he vacates and I move in from below, the slightly sunken nymph technique will be a winner. When he vacates and I enter the riffle from above, the floating nymph or spinner pattern may be most effective, especially in mid-to-late season. Note that the spinner is much easier to fish than the slightly sunken nymph downstream. That is, it is much easier to set the hook when you can see the clear outlines of the fish's mouth rise above the chop of the surface to take the jack-of-all-trades spinner.

True emergers. We use the term "true" emerger to distinguish any floating fly pattern that is neither a true floating nymph or a true floating dun or a true floating spinner. This category might include dun-like flies in which there is a large, upright wing, with the front part of the fly the color of the dun body while the rear portion of the fly is shaped and colored like a nymph shuck. One of our favorite such patters is the orange-biot-colored emerger sold by George Anderson's Yellowstone Angler shop. The back portion of the fly represents the highly segmented nymph shuck with short tails, while the front portion of the fly represents the dun-with-wings. This is deadly during the middle of the hatch for both the PMD and sulphur, with only slight differences in size.

Another type of emerger is one in which the wing has not yet unfolded to an upright position, but the fish can see a lighter dun body emerging from the nymphal shuck. Tom Travis' pattern is great for this type of fly. Note, however, that either type of emerger – unfolded wings with trailing shuck, or partially un-folded wings with trailing shuck – will represent only a brief period of time in the emergence of the mayfly. In typical mid-summer conditions with high temperatures, the actual hatch of the mayfly occurs rather quickly after the nymph finally secures its position in the meniscus. Many times I have stopped fishing to admire the emergence process. You can look straight down where the water touches your boots and, after your eyes adjust, you can see a black dot floating toward you. This is the floating nymph (or rather the dark wing-case of the nymph). Then, the black dot fairly quickly turns to a yellow dot as the dun emerges, then the yellow dots seems to suddenly have upright wings. The process from floating nymph to floating dun may happen very quckly, taking less than 2 feet of surface drift, with the unfolding-wing version of the dun occurring in the last 6 or 10 inches of float. Then, the true dun rides for several more feet before becoming airborne. Thus, the true emerger configuration of the mayfly may represent less than 5% of time from which the nymph locks itself into the film and the time the dun flies away into the clear mountain air.

Indeed, when we talk about the emergence of mayflies in terms of our earlier "probability distribution," we see that the slightly sunken nymph, as it is taking its several trips to the surface, may drift many feet downstream. This downstream movement of the slightly sunken nymph may or may not be less time-consuming than the downstream drift of the floating dun – yet, both types of position are much more lengthy (in time consumed or feet of water drifted) than the floating nymph. Still, *the floating nymph consumes more time than the true emergence event*. We haven't conducted real statistical studies of this, but our casual observations suggest that the probability of any one trout seeing a particular slightly-sunken nymph is greater than that of the trout seeing the floating dun, but the probability of seeing the dun is more than that of the trout seeing a floating nymph and more than that of the trout seeing a true emerger. *However, the floating dun can fly off at any instant, while the slightly-sunken or floating nymph cannot.* That is why the bulging or truly rising trout is taking many more nymphs than it takes duns. And that is why the slightly-sunken nymph technique or the floating nymph technique out-fishes the true dun or the true-emerger patterns. But, since you never know what the angler that previously fished over your fish has been using, it is important to have both true duns and true emergers in your arsenal.

13: The Imitations.

In this chapter we'll take a look at the fly boxes that Suzanne and I use on the Paradise Valley spring creeks, starting with the sub-surface patterns.

Sub-surface flies

1. <u>The pheasant-tail</u>. We've collected lots of real nymphs from the creeks and raised them in one of our aquariums. One of the most striking features of these nymphs is their segmentation. Not only is the segmentation obvious but, with the Baetis nymphs, there will be a couple of lower segments that are contrastingly light colored. While the main body color of the nymphs when they are mature (and beginning their multiple trips to the surface) varies widely, the wing-case typically is black when the emergence is ready to begin. So, the head area of the fly should be dark – yet, it is vitally important to have at least two different *body* colors -- dark vs. light – each with a dark wing-case.

The dark body version, which constitutes maybe 70% of the flies that we carry in the boxes, can best be imitated by Al Troth's tie – which foregoes the use of fibers to imitate legs. Legs may be an important triggering device for large mayfly nymphs or for stoneflies, but for the PMD and Baetis hatches, the key is for the fly to be skinny, especially so for the Baetis. We started using Al's flies in the early 1980's and each year our order for his flies kept growing. I would kid Al that I had to buy so many of his flies because you could catch only a dozen or so fish on each fly before the fly would come apart. And in the good ole' days, it was not unusual to go through a dozen of a particular size of olive pheasant tail in a single day.

Yes, there were lots of days when I would have more than a 100 hook-ups, but, back then, we fished long days. Back then, as now, we consider it a "good" day in which you average 8 hook-ups an hour through-out the course of the day -- although having a "good" day is not that unusual. True, a single hour here or there might result in 20 hook-ups, but it has not been possible to maintain that rate through the inter-hatch periods. And neither of us can take a full 12-14 hour fishing day anymore. But if we could tolerate the pain, exceeding 100 hook-ups in a day is now no more difficult than it was in the 1970's. The fish are more sophisticated because they see more sophisticated fishermen than in the 70's. But the improvement in flies, tackle, tippets, and techniques are at least a match for the increase in numbers of fishermen. Undoubtedly, the improvement in technique will continue. The day is not too far off when 9x on 1-weights will be used – we have already used 9x for "show-off" purposes.[36] But think of a tippet that is 33% thinner than 8x!!

The pheasant-tail patterns we use consist of, within each hook size, 8 types of pattern – the weighted dark PT on a heavy hook, the un-weighted heavy hook dark PT, the un-weighted light-wire-hook dark-colored PT, the un-weighted and treated-to-float light-wire-hook but dark-colored PT -- then these same 4 types tied with a light, natural PT fiber instead of dark olive dyed PT fiber. Almost all the fishing from season's start (when it stops snowing for a few days in March) through the November doldrums can be done with these 8 possibilities tied on 3 hook sizes – 16, 18, 20. However, the hook size refers to gape not length, and we can alternate between the use of traditional length shank (such as a Tiemco 101 hook) versus a short-shanked wide-gaped hook (such as a Dai-Ichi #1540 used by Al and, now, Lee). Note that every one of our nymph patterns entails a straight-eyed hook. This increases the effective gape of the hook and thus its hooking power.

My own nymph box (with a swinging leaf in the center and pure foam on all 4 portions of the box) has a whole side of one leaf devoted to weighted patterns; another whole side of a leaf is devoted to un-weighted but heavy hook patterns; a 3rd leaf has a collection of un-weighted PTs tied on fine wire hooks (plus some floating nymphs with hackle and some true "emergers"); and the 4th side of a leaf has all midges, scud, etc. See the photo below which shows only one of the leaf sides – the side with nothing but un-weighted PTs on regular wire hooks (not 1x fine high-riding floating nymphs).

All the patterns first developed by Al Troth used a relatively wide gape (for their length) and a straight-eye. Al taught us that hooking the quick-as-lightning "spitters" on the spring creeks requires a large gape with a very sharp hook. The diamond hook hone is one of our most important tools and must be used after every hook-up, after every missed fish, after every cleaning of the hook due to weed build-up, plus when you just feel like it. The sharp hook with

---

[36] The Power-Full brand line-up includes 9x, but it is very rarely imported into the States nowadays.

the wide gape, coupled with the nearly-invisible 8x, is what accounts for the high hook-up rate – assuming that you've chosen the right fly, the right distance to the micro-indicator (or lack thereof), the right fish to cast to from your position, and have made the perfectly accurate cast, then have struck before the spit-out occurs.

Al's pheasant-tail ties were so very different from the Sawyer-style nymph, with its heavy weighting of wrapped copper wire, and so very different from the hackle-tied un-weighted PTs of Skues, that it was easy to develop the slightly sunken nymph techniques that the spring creek trout saw so little of, until recently. Al's flies were so much narrower than the ungainly PTs we still see in most of the fly shops that it was natural for the arrogant rainbows to fall prey to our imitations. And Al's PTs garnered us lots of friends all over the world. Everywhere that we fished, we carried additional dozens of the flies to give as gifts. This practice started when one highly popular guide in Argentina said that he had never seen the famous Arroyo Malleo fished using these techniques. He would stand by my side for hours in wonderment as the trout would move to take the fly. As we were leaving, he said that a dozen of Al's flies would be the greatest "tip" he could ever receive. I think we gave him way more than that, and we felt a great loss when we left that country for the last time.

When Al developed Parkinson's, his fly tying eventually had to come to an end. The little red catalogues with the photos of his clients holding tremendous Beaverhead trout stopped being printed. And, like thousands of knowledgeable anglers all over the world, we were left with wondering "how long can we make the remaining dozens of Al's PTs last?" And, do we fish right down to the last dozen? Or save a bunch of them for posterity? We wound up saving several dozen; these will never be fished.

Al's great gift as a production fly tyer was not only his ingenuity at creating new ties like the Elk Hair Caddis and many others, but also his unequaled ability to tie a dozen flies that seemed so identical to each other that we wondered whether he had invented some new kind of tying machine (could there possibly be a patent outstanding?). Around the late 1990's we began to "interview" local and distant fly tyers. I would send them a sample of one of Al's flies then ask for them to tie a bunch, specifying the hook size and the materials, and ending with the request that the tyer send us a dozen of each particular pattern. After about a year, we were ready to give up -- no tyer consistently matched our samples. Then, Buzz Basini suggested we get to know Lee Kinsey. Lee runs an outfitter's service out of Livingston and, like some outfitters, ties in the winter to help offset the boredom of heavy snows and few fishing days. Indeed, I've learned that the best Livingston tyers are NOT skiers – thank Heaven.

All the sub-surface flies shown in this chapter are Lee's. We got to know one another quite well, since he has supplied many of the innovative flies in Buzz' shop on DePuy's. Time after time, I'd hear one of his neophyte-spring-creek-clients say – "Wow, I wonder what that guy's using?" And Lee would very softly say, "Oh, John's using the same blonde pheasant tail you're using." Incidentally, the blonde PT is much lighter than the normal PT which itself is much lighter than the olive PT. During the Baetis hatches in August, being able to use 3 color-change gradations is a wonderful thing.

The photographs show Lee tying several types of PT – varying in color combinations, the use of weight or not, and the type of hook. A Kinsey-tied Troth *weighted* olive PT is a true killer in the early season. The secret is to use, in addition to the large-gape hook, very fine black wire as weight within the thorax area, and to use very fine gold wire to accomplish the segmentation. These details were taught to us by, of course, Al Troth. The same fly in un-weighted configuration uses peacock herl in the thorax area. And this latter fly, tied on a Tiemco 101 and treated with something like Frog's Fanny or Fly Magic, is one of the best floating nymphs out there. There are many days when my natural progression of tactics on each fish causes me never to get to the floating nymph – no need. But I do enjoy fishing that hard to see fly and always will.

2. <u>Midge pupae and larvae</u>. The midge hatches are characterized by fairly frenzied feeding near or on the surface. Often, the angler switches to a midge pupa because the fish are bulging but the slightly sunken mayfly nymph is not working. We've also found that the midge hatches often seem to require fishing the slightly-sunken pupa down and across, rather than in the easier straight-upstream fashion. Maybe this is because of the simple fact that, as the mayfly hatch begins to wane, the midge hatch seems to start. The angler, by then, has fished through a whole section of stream and finds that it is easiest (less crowded) simply to turn around and begin fishing down through the water just vacated. Since many of these fish have been taken on the slightly sunken nymph, it's natural to switch patterns, but not necessarily techniques.

The midge pupa patterns are characterized by even skinnier bodies than the Baetis nymphs, with a head slightly wider than the body. We have *not* found it useful to put respiratory antennae, wing pads, or legs on the pupa, probably because the spring-creek midge pupae are significantly smaller than the pupae found on the various spring lakes in the region. It is also possible that the majority of spring creek midge pupae consist of those that Hafele and Hughes describe as "enclosed in a smooth, cylindrical puparium."[37] Nevertheless, we have not researched the midges as much as the mayflies, and, as spring creek techniques become more widely known, and the trout get more educated, these details may come to the fore.

It is also not clear whether any particular imitation purchased in one of the several fine area fly

---

[37] P. 190, Hafele and Hughes, 1981.

112

shops is intended to represent a pupa or a larva. That is, except for dimensions and coloration, several "pupariums" and larvae look about the same. Therefore, our current fly box selections contain just 4 types of pupae/larvae.

- The "miracle nymph", which is generally thought to represent the larva.

- The black biot pupa, which is generally thought to represent the pupa, with red thread or red wire used to present the segmentation.

- The traditional "brassie", which is generally thought to represent the pupa, but which, by virtue of its weight is usually fished well under the surface as if it were a larva.

- The "red" pupa, which some think represents the moment at which the pupa is transforming into the adult up within the surface of the water. Interestingly, several "red" pupa patterns available at the local shops, entail the use of a small red plastic bead at the head of the fly. The imitation looks realistic alright, but the bead serves to make it impossible for the imitation to float near or in the surface. We find the fly to be very useful, however, and it remains in our boxes.

3. <u>Scuds and Sow-bugs</u>. In this category, there is not much sophistication. Again, this may be due to the lack of research, and things could change in the future as the fishermen and the fish wise up. I wrote about Al Troth's scud pattern in a Summer, 1981 issue of *Fly Fisherman*. Back then, this was the only good scud pattern that existed. It was highly imitative, using a narrow strip of plastic freezer bag to represent the crustacean's back. Nowadays, the main imitation is called the flash-back scud, in which the dubbing is sparkle fiber and the back is tied with the same material as used in a flash-back pheasant tail. Incidentally, so long as the *flash-back* pheasant tail is tied in the correct proportions (with a skinny body and proper length tails), it is a good addition to your PT collection. Throughout the 1990's we carried both flash-back scuds and Troth scuds, but now we never see the latter in fly shops.

Sow-bugs are the least researched members of the sub-aquatic insects in the spring creeks.

We'll break out and tie on a sow-bug imitation perhaps only a couple of days of the year, when there is no mayfly or midge activity and when the scud is not working. This happens so infrequently that we are more likely instead to call it quits for the day, and go have an earlier-than-normal glass of wine. This too is likely to change as the methods and materials keep evolving. For now, we have found no need to go beyond Lee Kinsey's great sow-bug imitation, which appropriately emphasizes the prominent back-stripe of the insect.

Surface imitations.

1. <u>The mayfly dun</u>. So much has been written about the tying of mayfly duns that we can't add much to the discussion. Other things equal, however, little details do seem to matter. Once body and wing proportions are worked out, the fly-tyer should pay attention to imitating the real insect's segmentation. The use of stripped quill is important for such imitations, as is the use of goose or turkey biot (just as in the case of the popular goose biot midge pupa). Also, the proper use of tail fibers – few and widely spaced (and not very long) – will serve to help stabilize the fly and therefore allow the tyer to dispense with the use of hackle. Hackle fibers do a great job of floating the fly in the riffle sections of freestone streams, but the riffle sections of spring creeks are virtually flat compared with, say, the riffles of the Madison. As a result, the spring creek fisherman should pay special attention to the imitation's ability to ride flush in the surface film, not cocked up high like a Royal Wulff.

The flush-floating feature is present in the 4 main types of *dun* imitations that we use:

- <u>The thorax dun with hackle clipped off the underside of the thorax</u>. A thorax dun (similar to Marinaro's famous tie), when purchased from most fly shops, will have the winding of the hackle fully around the thorax, ahead of and behind the thorax upright wing, and above and below the thorax. The hackle protruding on either side of the wing (on TOP of the fly) doesn't seem to put off the fish. But the hackle protruding underneath the thorax will cause the fly to tip upwards and too backwards in a way that we and the fish find off-putting. Fortunately, the same fly-tying scissors you use for fashioning micro-indicators can be used for clipping the bottom portion of the hackle up close to the thorax of the fly. Do this before you treat the fly with floatant, then use Aquel, Frog's Fanny, or Dry Magic The result will be a fly that floats flush, yet takes only minimal treatment (with Frogs Fanny, to dry out the fibers) to float again after you land the fish. You can also experiment with how close to the thorax to clip the bottom hackle (clipping it not all the way to the thorax will cause the wing to tip somewhat backward in a pleasing manner, but without signaling that there is too much mass of an artificial something under the thorax. This partial-tipping trick can be heightened by cutting the underside hackle in a way that makes the number of remaining hackle fibers small in number (like legs rather than something that shouts "hackle, watch out!"). Once you begin to use your tying scissors this way on the stream, you'll never leave home without them.

The small thorax dun with a dark wing and quill body is a killer for the early season Baetis tricaudatus. Later in the year, when the second brood of that fly becomes the famous "sulphur", the same imitation, but with a segmented sulphur-colored dubbed body works just fine. It is even possible to color a quill-bodied fly with an orange waterproof marking pen.

- The Comparadun. This famous Caucci-Nastasi fly is a stand-out. It is a variant of the older Haystack, with no hackle and with deer hair fibers as the wings. The deer hair fibers are flayed out to the side to stabilize the fly in the proper position. Comparaduns come in many flavors. My very favorite BWO is a cul-de-canard (or CDC) comparadun instead of a deer-hair wing comparadun. It is important, however, for the CDC to be tied with leading edges that will stabilize the fly in the surface film (see Lee Kinsey's curved CDC emerger in the tying section). Most comparaduns pay little attention to segmentation, so it is important to look for ones that have a quill body or a body segmented with fine gold wire or thread. Tails can be regular tails or fibrous imitations of a portion of a trailing shuck. Our favorite PMD "dun" imitation is sold in Anderson's Yellowstone Angler and it's not meant to be a dun but rather an emerger (one of Rene Harrop's wonderful ties). It consists of a deer hair set of wings, an orange-biot segmented body, and fibers instead of tails (for the shuck). During the early days of the PMD, the Harrop emerger often out-fishes other dun-like imitations 2 to 1. We think it is because the biot-bodied "shuck" presents a much more segmented appearance than the typical dubbed body, and so the biot-body looks just as real as a dun's body (free of its shuck), rather than the emerging dun with attached shuck it was designed to imitate.

- <u>Swisher-Richards no-hackle</u>. This dun imitation was the only type of dun I used when fishing the Eastern limestoners during the 1970's. It was, and is, a truly innovative tie, which is often found poorly tied in many shops. The wings must be placed so that the bottom edges of the wings provide stability. Really good ones can be found in the Livingston area shops including Anderson's, Basini's Spring Creek Specialists (SCS), and Dan Bailey's. There are a couple of newer shops in town that I have not yet had the opportunity to visit. Bozeman also has some good shops, so don't hesitate to stop in on your way from the airport to Livingston. But spend some time looking for the right spring creek flies. And be forewarned that at most shops, except for SCS, you will have to sort through dozens of flies of a particular type in order to find a single dozen that are all properly proportioned.

  The yellow-bodied no-hackle competes with the comparadun as our favorite true dun during the season. The no-hackle, however, seems to have an advantage over the comparadun when it comes to imitating PMD spinner falls (see below). On the especially heavy PMD spinner falls that often occur on Nelson's during early evening (when you can still see to fish), this fly has produced many fond memories.

- <u>Parachute duns</u>. This type of tie solves the problem of riding flush in the surface film. However, its wing imitation, which serves the dual purpose of providing the post upon which the horizontally wound hackle is tied, doesn't really look much like a wing. Frankly, we think of the parachute dun as serving two types of non-dun purpose: First, it makes a great spinner imitation if you cut the post down to the point where it is serving simply as an indicator of the position of the fly. For this purpose, a white or gray winged post serves well during sunlight conditions, while an orange-colored post serves well during waning light, and a black post serves especially well during glare or flat-light conditions. The wings of the spinner are imitated by the hackle that emanates from the body.

  Second, the parachute dun also serves as a strike indicator when you use a nymph dropper. Yes, we have discussed earlier why the micro-indicator is preferred to the dropper method, but there are times when the micro-indicator doesn't work – such as when there is heavy glare or when particular trout are moving out of the way of even the smallest indicator, before they resume their feeding near or on the surface. In either case, most fish do not seem as put off by an indicator that itself is an imitation of a real fly. The problem, of course, is how do you tie on a dropper nymph using the very light tippets needed for sub-surface, finicky feeders? One answer is to use 7x G-Max tippet, with about a 24 inch length tied onto the bend of the hook of the floating-fly-indicator. This is about the minimum length of 7x that will not automatically break when you set the hook after seeing the indicator move.

2. <u>True emergers</u>. I use the word "true" in this context to point out an often-heard comment of anglers. Many times I will hear an angler say "I got him on an emerger." When asked whether their fly was floating or sub-surface, the angler will often say, "why, underneath, of course." This statement is supported by the fact that the angler is using a fairly good sized fluorescent green strike indicator. The angler seems to be thinking that this particular mayfly, hatching now (or in the pre-hatch period), accomplishes the partial or complete unfolding of its wings while underwater.

This mis-conception, I think, occurs because some commercially available nymph imitations are tied with partially unfolding wing cases. This can be an accurate imitation of a true emerger, in which the back half of the fly represents the nymphal shuck, while the front half represents an emerging dun with unfolding wings (and a dun-colored thorax). However, fishing such an imitation under the surface represent either a gap in the angler's knowledge, or, more likely, the angler has intentionally sunk the fly and is fishing it, well, as a nymph. While some types of mayfly are thought to unfold their sub-imago wings under the surface, although I am not aware of documented evidence on this belief, this is not the case with the major Ephemerella and Baetis flies on the Paradise spring creeks.

This fact has not stopped some angling artists from depicting PMDs with unfolded wings sub-surface. Indeed, there is a famous 1977 print by the gifted Eldridge Hardie, titled "Spring Creek", that shows a mayfly hatch on Armstrong's, with the beautiful Absaroka mountains above the water's surface, and many fine rainbow trout feeding <u>below</u> the surface on nymph-forms with unfolded wings. However, neither the PMD nor the Baetis unfold their wings beneath the surface, but rather in the meniscus. It is possible that some very small percentage of emerging duns die while attempting to emerge, and then sink. It is also the case that the spinners of some Baetis species swim below the surface to lay their eggs. But "emergers" of the spring creek mayflies do their emerging on, or rather in, the surface.

When it comes to tying good imitations, it is important to distinguish between emergers and floating nymphs. As I have indicated earlier, floating nymphs take up more floating time than does the actual emergence. So the probability distribution calls out for the angler to use a floating nymph rather than a nymph in the act of emerging into a dun. Nevertheless, some percentage of the population does not emerge successfully, or emerges slowly while floating a long way. This type of food can best be imitated by a floating tie, one in which the back portion of the imitation looks like a pheasant tail nymph while the front portion looks like a dun. We have several imitations that fit this bill, including a couple that are intended to have the "pheasant tail" portion of the fly suspended just under the surface while the "dun" portion floats on top of the surface. All of these imitations are "dry flies" in the truest sense and we use them when the slightly sunken nymph is not working on one or more particular fish. By "dry-fly" I mean that some part of the artificial fly floats on or in the surface film. Like all dry fly fishing, the use of emergers is best accomplished by casting down and across, and using the stop-cast to cause S-curves in the tippet. And like all dry-fly fishing, you can get good action without resorting to 8x, because, when you fish downstream, the fly arrives prior to the arrival of the tippet.

Our favorite emergers and floating nymphs include:

- The light-wire, floatant-treated PT, as discussed above.

- The Harrop emerger with PT or biot segmented bodies.

- The CDC with biot body or PT body, on either a straight hook or a curved hook. In the case of the curved hook biot-body (or PT body), only the thorax area of the fly should be treated with dry-fly floatant. That thorax, plus the wondrous properties of CDC, will keep the front half of the fly floating, while the nymphal body often will ride just under the surface.

- Troth emerging mayfly. This tie uses a brown, small diameter hackle feather tied in at the tail to simulate the nymphal shuck. It is a killer on the sulphur hatches.

3. <u>Spinner imitations</u>. As indicated earlier, our most successful spinner imitations have segmented bodies and float well down into the meniscus. Some of our favorite spinner patterns are shown in the photographs. But all of our spinners are best tied with quills for segmentation. As we noted in an earlier footnote, A.K.Best writes that...."A single quill is the closest thing to a perfect representation of the spinner body....(and) its floating qualities are astoundingly good.[38]

As you look through the photos of the imitations, and the accompanying recipes for materials and tying techniques, please remember that small details can be altered to achieve an unique appearance. When creating segmentation, for example, the tyer can alternate between extra-fine gold wire and extra-fine copper wire. The copper-wire segmentation can impart a more reddish color to a pheasant-tail nymph or floating imitation. Segmentation can also be achieved by using wider-than-normal olive thread, or red thread, etc. Also, when on the stream, you can modify the shape of floating flies by using your fly-tying scissors to cut down hackle, or wings. But try not to cut tails, since the result will often be a thick-looking truncated monstrosity. And cut sparingly at first, because it's easy to ruin a good floating imitation; and, although flies are still one of the greatest bargains in fly fishing (at $2-$3, when they cost $1.00 in the 1970's), the price is sure to keep rising as the best tyers must be compensated for their extraordinary talents.

The next several pages contain photographs of Lee Kinsey's ties of many of our "secret weapons." The tying instructions are included. The CD attached to the rear of the book contains over 75 color photographs of the tying process arranged with the instructions for each step in the process. Please download the PDF file on the CD to your computer and print out the color step-by-step photos so that you can have them right at your tying desk.

For computer neophytes, the way to use the CD is straightforward.

1) On a PC running any version of Windows, put the CD into the CD or DVD drive, then double-click on My Computer. There, look for your CD/DVD drive and double-click it. This will open a window showing what's on the CD. Find a file called "Fly Tying for the Rainbows of Paradise" and drag-and-drop the file to your desktop. You can then read the

---

[38] <u>A.K.'s Fly Box</u>, p. 131.

file (if your computer has a version of Adobe Reader, if not, you can download Adobe Reader for free from www.adobe.com). Simply double-click the icon that you created on your desktop to open the Fly Tying file. You can print out the entire Fly Tying section and place it in a binder for later use. Or, most efficiently, print out only those pages that you intend to carry down to your fly tying vise so you can look at them while you are tying.

2) On a Mac, well, just put the CD in and do what comes naturally.

Troth Un-weighted Pheasant Tail Nymph

Un-weighted Olive PT

Un-weighted Natural PT – Herl is still dark but body is much lighter than the Olive-dyed PT

Tying Instructions for Un-weighted PT

(Troth style). Tying is identical for Olive un-weighted PT except for the use of olive-dyed PT fibers and gold wire, instead of natural PT fibers and copper wire. *Note that Al Troth always used head cement on the materials at the end of each stage in the tying process. This greatly increases the number of fish you can catch on a fly before it begins to come apart.*

Materials list:

Hook: Dai-ichi 1640
Hook Sizes: 14-20
Thread: Uni-Thread 8/0 Black
Tails: Pheasant Tail
Ribbing: Ultra Wire XS or S, copper or gold
Body: 3 to 7 pheasant tail fibers, depending on size. Color is natural; dyed olive; or bleached
Wing: PT fibers folded over thorax area
Hackle: none
Weight: none
Post: none
Thorax: Peacock herl, trimmed underneath and sides, if necessary; bleached herl is used for the Blonde PT.

Important Details:

a) Trim peacock herl to make the thorax area only slightly larger than body.

b) Buy individual peacock tails (rather than strung herl), and size the herl before tying. Herl fibers near the base of the peacock tail are the smallest and finest. Most strung herl fibers are too thick for the smaller hook sizes.

Tying Instructions

1) Tie in the ribbing and the 3 to 5 PT fibers. Note that tail fibers are approximately one-third the length of the body. Do NOT make the tails too long!

2) Wrap the PT fibers forward, leaving room for the thorax (herl)

3) Wrap the ribbing forward, then take a few turns with the thread to aim the PT fibers toward the tail of the fly. This allows PT fibers to make a nice wing case after the herl is placed in the thorax.

4) Tie in the herl.

5) Wrap the herl forward.

6) Wrap the PT fibers over the herl to form the wing case, then whip finish.

7) Trim the herl under the fly and on the sides, if necessary. Very little bottom trimming and no side trimming are needed if the herl is sized properly for the size fly being tied. A size 16 is shown in the photo.

Note the large gape of this relatively heavy wire hook. This fly is meant to ride at about 6" or deeper in the water column. The same fly tied on a Tiemco 101 dry fly hook is meant to ride immediately under the film or, if treated, in the film.

Now, it is extremely important to pay attention to the *width* of your PT imitation depending on whether you are fishing a Baetis/sulphur hatch (think "skinny") or an Ephemerella hatch (think "wide"). The width of the PT can be controlled by a) the number of PT fibers you use in tying the fly, and b) the thickness of the peacock herl you use. In the next photo, we show the effect of differing numbers of PT fibers.

122

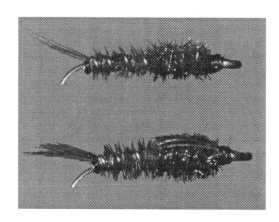

Both flies in the photo above are tied on a size 18 Tiemco 101 light-wire dry-fly hook. Both use olive-dyed PT fibers and small herl. The top fly is tied with 3 PT fibers; the bottom fly is tied with 7 fibers. The top fly also has undergone some trimming of the herl in the thorax area.

Troth-Kinsey Weighted Olive Pheasant Tail Nymph

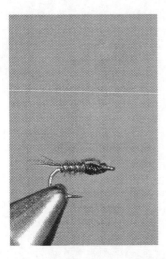

Tying instructions for the weighted pheasant tail nymph.

Photos show the Olive-dyed version. The natural PT version has the same black wire weighting for the thorax. Note that in Lee's version, peacock herl is NOT tied-in over the black wire weighting, in order to give the fly the nicest proportions. Also, there is no weight under the body, just the wire serving double-duty as weight and as thorax. This forward-weighting offsets the extra weight of the hook bend, allowing the fly to ride more naturally in my view.

Materials list:

Hook: Dai-ichi 1640
Sizes: 14-20
Thread: Uni-Thread 8/0 Black
Tails: 3-7 PT fibers, olive or natural
Ribbing: Ultra-Wire, S or XS, gold or copper. Note that you can also use the copper colored wire both as ribbing and as thorax weight (much as in the Sawyer method).
Body: 3-5 Pheasant tail fibers
Wing: wing case of PT fibers
Hackle: none
Weight: Ultra-Wire wrapped many times at thorax.
Post: none
Thorax: Wire weighting

Instructions: Use same procedure as for unweighted PT. However, instead of peacock herl, use the black Ultra Wire for the thorax. Since the wire thorax will not be built-up on top of the thorax as in the case of the herl, make sure the wrapped-over PT fibers (to form the wing-case) are done with some slack above the black-wire thorax.

Note: Al Troth used lead wire for weight in the thorax, then wrapped herl around this weight. This is quite doable in the larger sizes.

124

Black Goose-Biot Midge Pupa

Tying instructions for midge pupa.

This is the most popular pupa in the fly shops, but don't be afraid to experiment with other versions. The fly is tied on a light scud hook, but the hook still is heavier than a typical dry fly hook. So, remember to use an extremely small micro-indicator close to the fly if you wish to suspend it high in the water column. Note also that the head of the fly is relatively narrow, indicating a "puparium" of the sort discussed earlier. The tyer should feel free to substitute a larger dubbed head.

Materials list:

Hook: Tiemco 2487
Sizes: 16-22
Thread: Uni-Thread 8/0 black
Tails: none
Ribbing: Ultra-Wire XS red or gold or copper
Body: Turkey or Goose Biot. Color: Black, olive, or white
Wing: none
Hackle: none
Weight: none
Post: none

Thorax: Thread wrapped to make head slightly wider than body. Be sure to get the length and width of the head correct in relation to length of body (as in photograph), unless you purposely wish to use a broader dubbed or peacock herl thorax..

125

Instructions for midge pupa:

1) Tie in thread and red-wire ribbing. Make sure these start well around the curvature of the hook.

2) Tie in goose or turkey quill at slightly around the bend of the hook.

3) Wrap quill so that fibers flair to the sides; leave just enough room for thread-head. Note position of tag-end of biot to allow space for head.

4) Wrap wire ribbing forward; secure; then build up the thread head and whip finish. Note the lack of breathing fibers.

Lee's Sow-Bug

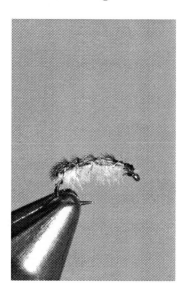

Hook: Tiemco 2487
Sizes: 16-20
Thread: Uni-Thread 8/0 black
Tails: none
Ribbing: Ultra Wire, small, copper or gold
Body: Bleached Peacock Herl
Wing: none

Weight: none
Hackle: none
Post: none
Thorax: not different from body
Other: Back covering of 4-6 PT fibers,
natural

Tying instructions for sow-bug

The sow-bug has a distinctive stripe down
its back. Lee uses PT fibers to imitate both
this stripe and the overall carapace or back-
covering of the insect

Tying instructions:

1) Tie in copper or gold ribbing; tie in
    about one-third of the way down the
    curve of the hook.

2) Tie in PT fibers at same place
    around curve of hook

3) Tie in bleached herl, 2 fibers, along
    shank of hook, ending at back of
    hook, where the wire and PT fibers
    are tied in. Remember to use herl
    nearer to the eye or tip of the
    peacock tail, rather than the base of

the tail. These tip fibers are thicker than those at the base.

4) Wrap the strands of herl to the front and secure.

5) Bring the PT fibers over the body toward the front and secure. The PT fibers should be covering the whole back and pushing the herl fibers down on either side of the hook.

6) Wrap the ribbing wire to the front, creating 4 or 5 body segments, depending on hook size. Whip finish. Note that, if herl size is chosen properly, no trimming is needed, except possibly on sides. Choose a herl size so that the herl width, as shown in the photo, is approximately one-half of the gape of the hook.

Kinsey Thorax Dun
(PMD/sulphur/olive)

Tying instructions for thorax dun

There are several keys in tying this fly, including some differences from traditional thorax duns:
- The use of dubbing to help with the splitting of the tail fibers
- The use of Micro-Fibbets for tails (but shorter than for a spinner pattern)

- The use of turkey biots for the body
- The use of turkey flats for the wing(s)
- The use of bleached grizzly super saddle hackle

At the end, we also outline some specifics in preparing the turkey flats when making the wing.

Materials List:

Hook: Dai-ichi 1310
Sizes: 16-20
Thread: Uni-Thread 8/0 yellow (or light cahill); olive
Tails: Micro-Fibbets (4) – ginger or dun
Ribbing: none
Body: Turkey Biot -- sulphur or olive color
Wing: Tan or light gray turkey flats
Hackle: Bleached grizzly super saddle-hackle
Post: none
Dubbing: for tail-splitting and thorax area – Beaver Dubbing, sulphur, yellow, or olive (Rocky Mountain Dubbing)

Tying instructions:

1) Leave the tying thread sticking straight out of the tail. Then, tie a dubbing ball at tail of hook, then tie in 4 Micro-Fibbets over the dubbing.

2) Use the tying thread tag-end (which was left sticking straight out the tail) to separate the 4 tails into 2 on each side of the dubbing ball.

3) Tie in the turkey quill and run thread to front of hook.

4) Tie the quill forward to form the body.

5) Form the wing out of the turkey flat (see separate photos and instructions at end) and tie in the wing. This is done by a) tying in the butts at the front of the hook, b) taking a couple of turns of thread at the back of the wing; c) taking 2 or 3 parachute turns of the thread at the base of the wing and d) finishing off the thread behind the wing.

6) Tie in the bleached grizzly hackle behind the wing.

7) Wrap the dubbing behind and in front of the wing.

8) Take 2 wraps of hackle behind the wing and 2 or 3 wraps in front; finish off and whip-finish.

9) Two types of cutting are now required (go slowly, the fly is already tied):

a) Cut the wing so that it assumes the shape of a slightly tilted backward mayfly wing – a short horizontal cut at the top of the wing (not all the way across), followed by an angled cut from the end of the first cut down toward the tail of the fly.

b) Clip a V-shaped notch out of the hackle underneath the hook. The result should be that the hackle fibers project out from the fly and slightly downward. See the photo. There is no need to clip hackle near the wing.

Instructions for forming turkey flat wing:

a) Hold turkey flat with concave side upward.

b) Tear off the webbing and separate the section to be formed into a wing (in the photo, this is the first set of fibers on the left side of the flat, still facing concave side up).

c) Size the section to be torn off at twice the width of the wing to be fashioned. Then, hold the section between the fingers of your left hand and tear off the rest of the flat using your right hand.

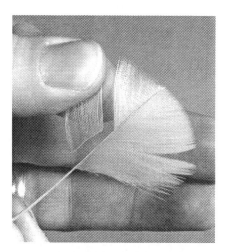

d) It is important to keep the fibers flat in your left fingers for the next step.

131

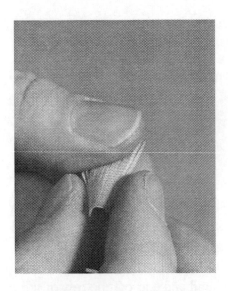

e) Fold the fibers in half in the
    direction shown.

f) This creates the symmetrical wing as
held by your thumb and fore-finger of
the right hand.

Lee's Clipped-Hackle Spinner

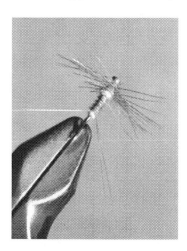

Tying Instructions for Spinner

The keys to tying this fly are the micro-fibbet tails (longer than for the dun), the biot body, and the dubbing at the thorax.

Materials list:

Hook: Dai-ichi 1310
Sizes: 16-20
Thread: Uni-Thread 8/0 olive or yellow (light cahill)
Tails: Micro-Fibbets, 2 each side, separated by tail dubbing ball; tail color is dun, to match hackle

Ribbing: none
Body: Turkey Biot, PMD color or Rust
Wing: none; hackle serves this purpose
Hackle: Super saddle-hackle, medium gray
Post: none
Thorax: Beaver Dubbing by Rocky Mountain Dubbing; same color used to separate tails; sulphur yellow or rust

Tying instructions:

1) Attach the thread to the hook, wind down to tail and put in the tail dubbing ball. Tie in the tail fibers AFTER the dubbing ball is in place (see instructions for the thorax dun).

2) Make the tails longer than for the dun; typically 50% (or more) longer than the body as in the photo. Use the thread to separate the tails (2 on each side). Tie in turkey biot in front of the tail ball, then wind the biot to the front, leaving room for the thorax area.

3) Tie in a single super-saddle hackle, then construct the dubbed thorax (somewhat thicker than the body but not too thick).

4) Wrap the hackle forward and tightly to the dubbed thorax, approximately 5 turns.

5) Trim the top and bottom of the hackle so that there is a "v" cut-out on the top and an inverted "v" cut-out on the bottom. Whip-finish.

The finished fly should float flush in the surface film.

Lee's Curved CDC Emerger

Tying the curved emerger:

The keys to this fly are the biot body for better resistance to the fly sinking, and the "cheeks" on the CDC that flare out on either side of the body to help stabilize the fly in the surface film. Note how these "cheeks" are missing on most commercially-tied CDC duns.

Materials list:

Hook: Tiemco 2487 (Note that this hook not only provides the curved body but also is sufficiently heavy to cause the body to break through the surface film. Treat only the thorax area with dry fly spray or ointment.
Sizes: 16-20
Thread: Uni-Thread 8/0 yellow (Light Cahill)
Tails: Zelon fibers, rust or brown, to simulate the lower half of the nymph body. Keep these a short as that of tails on a Baetis nymph.
Ribbing: none
Body: Turkey Biot, mahogany
Wing: 2 natural CDC feathers, natural grey
Hackle: none
Weight: none
Post: none
Thorax: Beaver Dubbing, sulphur yellow or light olive

Tying instructions:

1) Tie in the thread and the Zelon for the "tails"

2) Tie in the turkey biot

3) Wrap the biot to the front, leaving enough room for the thorax (about 5 wraps on this size 16)

4) Tie in two CDC feathers as shown.

5) After tying in the feathers, fold the webby ends back along the <u>sides</u> of the fly as shown

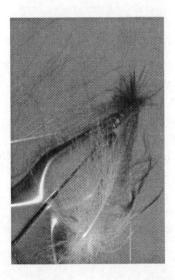

6) This photo shows another view of how the webby ends of the CDC feathers are folded back on either side of the fly.

7) Dub the thorax area and whip finish. Note that not very much dubbing is needed because the folded back CDC feather (after wrapping them with thread) already provides a built-up thorax area. After whip-finishing, cut the folded-back CDC feathers to create the "cheeks" on either side of the fly.

8) Finished fly shows the short CDC fibers along each side (right behind the thorax) that stabilize the fly in the surface film.

Miracle Nymph

Tying instructions:

This is a really simple tie but it is important to keep the proportions slim and with the proper number of segments. The finished product will tend to turn grayish in water, as is shown in the photo above .

Materials:

Hook: Tiemco 2487
Sizes: 18-20
Thread: Uni-thread 8/0 black
Tails: none
Ribbing: Ultra Wire, XS, gold

Body: White floss (single strand)
Head: Black thread

Instructions:

1) Tie in gold wire.

2) Choose only a single strand of floss (usually floss has 4 strands).

3) Tie in the floss at the same place as the gold ribbing – about 1/3 to 1/2 around the bend of the hook.

4) Wrap the floss forward being careful to lay it flat with little overlapping. Cut off the floss leaving enough room for the thread head.

5) Tie the head slightly wider diameter than the body, in the width shown. Whip finish. (Note that a version of the Miracle Nymph can be tied using <u>white turkey biot</u> and the same gold wire or black wire or black thread for segmentation. This fly does NOT turn gray in the water and is useful over trout that have become used to store-bought "miracle nymphs.")

Lee's Indicator Fly – HiVis PMD Parachute

The truth is that many fishermen will never be able to see the mini-micro-indicator needed to fish the sunken fly on 8x to difficult fish in August and later. For these fishermen, it is quite acceptable to use a fairly large "indicator" fly with a 24 inch segment of high-quality 7x tied to the bend of the hook on the indicator fly. In the early months of the season, there will be times when a trout takes the indicator fly. But the main purpose of the indicator fly is that the trout will think the floating fly is the offering, and the trout will continue to feed under the indicator fly, confidently sucking in the artificial nymph or pupa. During the tough times later in the year, this won't work on most of the trout in the spring creeks. But it's worth a try for the very near-sighted fisherman. The smaller size 18 or 20 indicator fly works best. And a few fish a day are better than nothing.

<u>Tying the indicator fly:</u>

<u>Materials list:</u>

Hook: Tiemco 100
Sizes: 16 to 20
Thread: Uni-thread 8/0 olive or sulphur
Tails: Micro-Fibbets
Body: Turkey Biot, olive, or sulphur
Ribbing: none
Dubbing: for thorax, olive or sulphur
Hackle: Bleached grizzly hackle
Post: Antron, orange

1) Tie in thread and tail fibers. No need to split the Micro-Fibbets, since the parachute hackle provides great stability.

2) Tie in the Antron post at the spot indicated, leaving room for the dubbed thorax. Then use the tying thread to wrap several turns

vertically (up, then down) on the post, to transform it into a stiff column. Make sure the wrapped portion of the post is high enough to accommodate the wrapping of the hackle and the dubbing of the thorax.

3) Tie in the turkey biot at the tail.

4) Wrap the biot forward to end immediately behind the post.

5) Tie in the bleached grizzly hackle behind the post and with a wind of thread at the base of the post.

6) Dub the thorax area.

7) Wind the hackle around the post, ending at the bottom front of the post.

8) Whip finish the head, then trim the post to the size shown. The photo is of a size 16 fly. Choose hackle that is slightly smaller than shown here, so that the extended hackle fibers do NOT reach all the way to the end of the fly.

Note that the bleached grizzly hackle provides what Lee regards to be a better color for the PMD/Sulphur flies than ordinary ginger. In the color CD you'll see the effect of the bleaching and the resulting dramatic transformation of the grizzly hackle.

Details matter

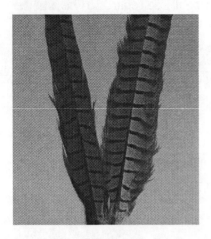

Note how much darker is the olive-dyed pheasant tail compared to the natural pheasant tail. Lee also ties a "blonde PT" using natural PT and a bleached peacock herl thorax.

The bleached peacock herl is on the left (in the lower photo left), compared with a

regular peacock tail in the middle. The right-hand herl in the picture is called a peacock "sword" and its fibers are especially small, for use on size 20 and 22 PTs.

This storage box shows some of Lee's sow bugs, white larvae, black-biot pupae, and various sizes of PT with size 24 in the upper left corner and size 16 in the lower right corner. These PTs, all un-weighted on Tiemco 101 hooks, constitute about 50 dozen flies – enough to last us a whole season and part of the next.

Other very useful patterns

Swisher-Richards no-hackle dun

Harrop emerger – he calls it the Biot Captive Dun (p. 196, Trout Hunter)

Foam-top floating nymph – essentially Tom Travis' emerger, but with turkey biot as the body instead of pheasant tail. Tying instructions are like those for the indicator fly, except for foam in place of Zelon post.

Troth emerging midge – Spring Creek Specialists carries a version of this fly. A killer during the midge hatches of late July and August. See the tying CD for tying instructions.

Troth emerging mayfly – you probably won't be able to find any more of these, but if you do, buy them out. The hook is #22 wide gape. Great during the tough Sulphur hatches. See the tying CD for tying instructions.

Orange-biot-bodied "emerger" (courtesy Anderson's Yellowstone Angler)

CDC quill-bodied dun – notice that this particular tie doesn't have the CDC flaired to the side (see the photos of tying the curved-body emerger discussed earlier). Thus, the fly is less stable than it should be.

Troth scud -- see fly-tying CD for instructions.

The sign at the old barn at Betty's Riffle, site of the Spring Creek Specialists shop.

Nelson's in the "old days", before the removal of the old corral
and the installation of the wing dams to improve flow.

Mother, father and 5 cygnets on DePuy's.

Male Baetis tricaudatus -- the "sulphur."

Male PMD spinner.

Male Pale Morning Dun.

14. Game Plan.

We've covered a lot of ground in these pages, and we've taken care to repeat in several places the things that are especially important. In this chapter, we try to give the angler a sense of how to *prepare* to fish the spring creeks. Go with a guide your first few times, for sure. Your eyes simply won't be ready for this business if it's literally your first time fishing such rich, difficult waters. And if you only get to fish the spring creeks a couple of days each year, then find a guide that suits your style of fishing and stay with that person for a long number of years (being sure to reserve his/her time well in advance of your annual Montana pilgrimage). Follow the guide's advice with regard to terminal tackle and all that. But always think about how you might alter your rig, your fly, your tactics, to solve a particular problem. And, especially, try to use some of the tactics you have learned on these pages, when your guide is off tending to another member of your party.

Do this "self-guiding" when you are feeling especially insightful, but only if you have confidence in your ability to cast accurately at close distances. Otherwise, your failures will only reinforce the view that "this is too tough to do on my own." So, when it comes to preparing for your trip to the spring creeks, this is where it starts -- with casting practice.

Casting. This topic cannot be divorced from the topic of leader/tippet construction, line weight, rod choices and other "tackle" issues. It also cannot be separated from the issue of learning how to cast before you learn how to fish. Far and away, the big failure of all newcomers to the creeks is that they think they are learning how to fish when, in fact, most of their day is spent learning how to cast. They do really *very little fishing*, since most of their casts are spent missing their intended target, putting down other fish, and/or educating eligible fish to the "artificial behavior" of their offerings.

Learn how to cast before the first day on the stream with the expensive guide. Do this by buying or borrowing a 2-weight outfit and constructing a "practice" set-up with respect to leader, tippet, and fly. Try to get a longer rod than is found in most catalogues under the category of "2-weight." It's appalling, but most manufacturers seem to believe that 2-weights are used only on small, brushy Eastern streams. So, we see lots of 7 foot, 2-weight fly rods, a few 8 foot, 2-weights, and no 8.5 foot 2-weights. The longer rod length is essential to achieving the high tip speeds needed to turn over a 16-foot leader/tippet combination (in the wind). The Livingston creeks, thank Heaven, are wide enough and clear enough of streamside high vegetation that you can always find a spot where your back-cast is not a problem. So, practicing at home on your wide-open lawn is just fine. And by so doing, you'll find that you can control the light-line-but-long-leader combination with more ease by employing a longer fulcrum. The extra 6 inches of the 8.5 foot rod make a big difference over that of the 8 foot rod. If there were a 9-foot 2-weight that was light enough and soft enough for our tastes we'd probably be using it by now. But finding the 8.5 foot 2-weight, especially in a 2-piece rod, is tough. There are a few 3-piece such rods and a 5-piece such rod, but no 8.5 foot 2-weights in 2-piece design. Some anglers think that 3-piece rods handle better than 2-piece rods, so the shortage of 2-piece, long 2-weights may not be a problem. And, fortunately, our older Winston 8.5 foot 3-weights handle a 2-weight very nicely. But, as we indicated earlier, Winston currently makes this rod in a 3-piece configuration. Please note that, in finding the right rod, you can find several 3-weight rods that will also handle a 2-weight line well. This will be far easier than finding a true 8.5 foot 2-weight.[39]

Note that the use of a 2-weight rod is quite in dispute among knowledgeable spring creek fishermen. Many of them do not accept that using 8x is a critical part of success. I think that many of these anglers do quite well without using 8x, have tried it with their 3 and 4 weight rods and line, have broken off lots of fish, and have therefore concluded that it is neither necessary nor desirable. Frankly, I think that these skilled anglers are happy with their 20 or 30 fish per day, and have not even imagined how their success could be doubled! Others are getting it, however. For example, Buzz Basini, in the elite of dry fly purists, knows that downstream casting using 7x is critical to his segment of our sport. And he knows that hooking and landing large spring creek trout on 7x cannot be done consistently with a 4-weight line – he uses a 3-weight exclusively. He also agrees that lighter tippets are needed for sub-surface imitations and that therefore, if I am going to use 8x tippet, I am much better off learning how to control a 2-weight. My general rule of thumb is that 8x requires a 2-weight, 7x requires a 3-

---

[39] Cabela's SLi 8.5 foot 3-weight in 2-piece design does very well with the 2-weight as does Winston's 8.5 foot 3-weight. However, the Cabela's SLi line of rods is missing from their 2009 catalogue. Early in 2009 I researched all the major manufacturers and found only a single 8'6" 3-weight rod in a 2-piece configuration – the Redington RS4. There are several companies that sell such a rod in a 4-piece or 5-piece configuration.

weight, and that 6x can be cast with a 4 or even a 5 weight line.

The difficulties associated with casting a 2 or 3 weight line, in the wind, on the spring creeks, are greater than most would expect. Rene Harrop, the Master of the Henry's Fork, writes in his new book, Trout Hunter, that

"Certain conditions produce a need for a specialized setup that may deviate from what we normally prefer to use. An example are the slow-action rods matched with light, 2- or 3-weight lines that have come into fashion for Spring Creek-type fishing…..Add a stiff breeze, however, and they quickly become less-than-effective tools in the hands of all but the most experienced and accomplished fly casters."

He then goes on to suggest using a 5 or 6-weight with 6x in such conditions. Rene is essentially right in this paragraph, except that he overestimates the difficulty in learning to cast a 2-weight with a long leader/tippet combination. It is not easy and especially not easy to become extremely accurate with the rig in the wind. But it is only "extremely difficult" if the caster sticks to the old way of casting with a slow stroke. And no one who has mastered the high-tip-speed needed for fishing the 2-weight in the wind, once he begins to appreciate the benefits of 8x tippets, will ever go back to the old ways.

We have noted earlier that the reel for the 2-weight rod should be a click-drag, if at all possible. We've experimented with many disc drag reels by all the major manufacturers and find that there is usually too much inertia on the drag at the moment of the strike and the first rush of the fish after feeling the hook.[40] You may be able to find some acceptable click-drag reels on the secondary market (e.g., Ebay™) – and Abel still lists in their 2009 catalogue the TR reels that we use. All things equal, it's nice to have the reel designed for a larger line than the 2-weight (e.g., for a 4 or even 5 weight line). This will result in fly line being wound over more backing and therefore at a greater diameter. Large arbor (tall and "skinny") reels accomplish the same thing, keeping the fly line in large loops that will prevent curls or kinks. Under no circumstances should your reel have a diameter of less than 3", even if the manufacturer sells a good quality small diameter reel. The extra weight of the large diameter reel will not upset your

---

[40] An exception might be the Ross Evolution, with which we are currently experimenting. It appears to have a light enough drag to protect the 8x tippets, but only a summer of hard use will confirm this.

casting accuracy in the least.

Start your set-up by having an 18" to 2-foot butt section of 20-lb Maxima (clear) butt material tied to the end of your fly-line. Do not use loops at the end of your fly line – it will destroy the needed accuracy (targets of less than 1-foot in diameter, in the wind). Have the store person tie on the butt section with a needle-knot (or do it yourself if you have young eyes). Now we'll repeat the leader/tippet formula we use: Buy a 9-foot, 7x knotless tapered leader, and cut off 18" of the butt portion of the leader. Tie this to the 2-foot butt section of Maxima. Then, cut off maybe 1 foot of tippet section and tie on a 2-foot section of transition 7x. Then tie on a 4 foot section of 8x tippet. You now have 14.5 feet of butt/leader/transition/tippet. This is the *minimum* length of leader/tippet you'll be fishing with on the spring creek once you learn how to cast the rig. Onto the tippet of this rig, tie on a size 18 pheasant tail (un-weighted) and clip off the hook (break it off, don't just bend down the barb). You don't want the hook getting caught on the grass or on your family members. Tie on a micro indicator (as per the earlier photographs) about 18" up from the fly. Then learn how to cast this outfit to a 9" dinner plate between 20 feet and 30 feet in front of your toes.

As we have discussed earlier, no leader/tippet recipe we have seen uses tippets much longer than 24-26" or so. Nor do hand-tied knotted leaders sold in some of the better fly-shops. Nevertheless, you should not use the recipe we give here without trying your own recipe in which you simply replace the short tippet with a longer one. Your own casting style, with a very slight modification might also work. Start out with your own recipe and a tippet one-foot longer than usual. Then, lengthen the tippet until you can handle one 5 feet in length with an un-weighted nymph and a mini-micro-indicator. This will be the real test of your casting style.

Also, practice in the wind; don't just go out on the lawn on a bright windless day. Better yet, find a stream close to home with some trout in it and practice casting this slightly-sunken nymph rig to those trout. Concentrate on learning how to cast. Don't mess around with tactics. Learn how to cast this dry-fly-like rig first, with the long tippet set-up and with the wind-resistance of the micro-indicator. Learn how to make the cast accurately with and without a reach cast. Don't mess around with learning hook-casts, you'll rarely need them. An accurately presented reach cast, however, will be vital on the spring creeks, and the reach portion of the cast is almost as important as the accuracy of the cast.

Reaching proficiency with this rig will not be done in a couple of half hour sessions. If you don't have time for this, then take up some other aspect of fly-fishing. True proficiency will arrive only with many days on the stream. When I wrote that it took me a whole summer to learn how to cast a 2-weight, I was referring to truly pin-point accuracy in the wind, with hooks in my cast (right and left-handed), along with the reach-cast. And I was referring to being able to achieve this same accuracy with the added complication of a #8 split-shot clamped on about 12-14 inches up from the fly (and with the strike indicator being slightly larger than micro, placed up at the 48" distance from the fly). Recall that, in this game, the ability to make terminal tackle changes frequently are part of the ability to change tactics frequently. When you can stand in one spot and cast to a half dozen fish using a half dozen tactics, and do this within a 15 minute period of time, you will have arrived.

As we have indicated earlier, it is also extremely important to realize that *the 2-weight line, the extremely long tippet in 8x, the change in casting technique, and the use of an almost invisible fly-indicator, are all part of an integrated package* that you should learn in order to do really well on the spring creeks. Many times over the years I have tried to teach these methods to friends who are experienced anglers, and the more experienced they are, the tougher time they have. If I leave them alone on the creek for a while, when I get back I'll find that their tippet is back down to 24" (and they'll break off the next fish). Or, they'll be using 7x in August and wondering why they are hooking very few while I'm having a blast. Or, I'll teach them using one of my own fly rods, with me standing at their side all day. The next year, when I join them on the creek, they'll be using a 3-weight with their 8x, instead of a 2-weight and wondering why they are breaking off fish left and right. It all fits together. Take advantage of these 40 years of experience.

Graduating from casting the long leader/tippet combo to the same combo with *weight* added is tough. Learn the weightless cast first, the one you'll be using the most when employing the deadly slightly-sunken nymph tactic. Then, and only then, learn how to cast the weighted nymph. The problem with the weighted rig is that it <u>cannot</u> be done well or consistently using the standard casting stroke. In the "standard" stroke, taught at all the fly-fishing schools, the caster learns to have lots of fly line out through tip. The forward cast and the back cast are in the same plane vertically and horizontally. The instructor tells the student to "wait" while the back-cast unfolds, then come forward using an accelerating force, then <u>stop</u> as the cast unfolds toward the target. This may be fine when you are in a situation where you have lots of fly line to wave around. The more fly line out there the easier it is to straighten out even long leader/tippet combinations. But using 30 feet of fly line, plus 14-16 feet of leader/tippet, on the spring creek means only that a) you miss your target and b) you lay the line down over other fish between you and your target.

Maybe the problem still resides with the old saying "fishing fine and far off." I don't know why this saying developed, but it's wrong for the spring creeks. You have to learn how to fish "fine and close-in." Every day on the creeks I meet up with at least one caster that demonstrates he can cast fine and far off, and proceeds to do so all day, with little success. What's more, when the fine and far off caster is a friend of mine, and I'm trying to teach him/her how to cast accurately at short distances in the wind, the inevitable problem is that old habits are hard to break. Also, while the caster might eventually learn how to cast the long-leader/light-tippet combo without any weight, when the split shot is added all hell breaks loose. "Waiting" for the back-cast to unfurl simply doesn't work with a split shot on an 8x tippet. You'll create a greater number of complex knots in your leader and tippet than you thought possible.

So, before you come out to the spring creeks, learn the weightless long-leader technique first (remembering that you have to do it without a lot of fly line out past the tip). Then try to learn the weighted fly technique next. Most importantly, learn from the outset that, whether the fly is weighted or not, you have to change two important things about your casting technique. First, you do NOT make the front cast and the back cast within the same plane. Second, you do NOT lock your wrist and use only your forearm as taught in some casting schools.

    a.   <u>The plane of the fly during the forward-backward strokes</u>. To get this point, it helps to envision the "spring-creek cast" as being made in an oval manner. If you are a right-hander, think about making your back cast further to the right than your forward cast. Sometimes, for some people, it also helps to think about the back cast as being made further to the right and *lower* than the front cast. The overall cast is made in an oval fashion with the plane of the oval tilted so that the edge of the back-cast is lower than the edge of the front-cast. Think about accelerating the front cast to a "stop", just as you were taught in casting school, but make that fly line and leader roll forward and straighten out *well above the water*. Sometimes I have to tell the student to aim his/her fly 4 or 5 feet above the 1-foot square "target" on the surface of the water. Otherwise, the acceleration of the fly line to make it straighten out in front of you results in the tip of the fly line slapping the water.

b. The use of the wrist. Another thing to remember is that, normally, when you have lots of fly line waving around in the air, you will lose control if you start bending your wrist back and forth. This is why the casting schools tell you to keep your wrist "locked" and to use your forearm to rotate around a fixed elbow position (i.e., your elbow close to your rib cage serves as a fulcrum). This instruction makes sense when you have, say, 30 feet of fly line out there. But when you are casting "fine and close-in", you simply can't get enough "tip speed" to control only 10 feet of fly line. So learn to use your wrist and don't be afraid to have a casting "loop" that is anything but small and tight. Casting our rig with a 2-weight in the wind is not meant to be pretty. Indeed, I often concentrate on having continual contact with the 10 feet of fly line, by using an oval stroke in which there really isn't a back-cast versus forward-cast, just a continuous oval pattern to the path of the fly-line-tip. This won't work for everyone – just do whatever you need to do in order to:

1) Straighten out all of the fly line plus all of the leader, but still have S-curves in the tippet. Often this requires a "stopping" of your cast at the very end of the forward-cast, in order to have the tippet bounce back toward you in the needed S-curves. Or, you can overshoot your target by "shooting" line past the target, then use your left hand (if a right-hander) to "feather" the cast back toward you. I do this so much on the spring creeks that I forget that I don't need to do it on our major rivers such as the Missouri.

2) Have the whole "cast" unfurl well above the water so that there is absolutely no slapping of the fly line tip on the surface.

3) When needed, end the cast with a "reach" to one side or the other. The reach cast will be used whenever there is faster or slower water between you and the drift line in which your target is feeding. For example, if the current is flowing from your right to your left, and if the trout is feeding in slower water on the other side of the main flow, then cast down and across to the

fish, and end the cast with a reach to the right. This way the faster current can carry the fly line downstream without affecting the fly as much (giving you a somewhat longer drag-free float).

Finally, try NOT to use a mend while fishing the spring creeks. We see guides, those without much spring creek experience, telling their clients to mend upstream after the cast. But, *this is not the Madison*. A mend simply creates a brief pause in the correct downstream drift of the fly. The guide is trying to get you to achieve a good float, but achieve this float with the <u>reach cast</u> – and know that there is no fisherman good enough to get a truly drag-free float that is much more than 3 feet or so in length. A mend may be needed when casting at distance, but the mistake is casting at distance to begin with. Don't make long casts; don't expect long drag-free floats; pick up the line and re-cast when you've achieved, say, a 3 foot float, and don't take the chance of having the fly drag for several inches at the end of an otherwise perfect cast. Think short, small, and efficient. Think a small number of casts before stopping to assess your position. This is NOT the Madison.

<u>The vest</u>. Details matter in spring creek fishing. It's not the construction of the vest that matters so much as what's in or on the vest. In particular, you should have your essential tools readily available. In the photograph below, note that the snippers, the fly-tying scissors, the pliers with a flat, no teeth design (to bend down barbs), the forceps for pinching on the tiny #8 split shot, and the diamond hone are all on their own retractors (we favor the Simms design for its indestructibility). The fly floatants (Aquel and Dry Magic) along with the sections of strike-indicator are in one pocket, while the split-shot and Xink are in another. Oh yes, the sections of strike-indicator reside outside of the plastic wrapper in which they are sold. No need to waste time pulling the pieces of indicator out of the package then putting them back inside the package each time you place a new micro-indicator on your tippet. This is very important because you will be doing three kinds of continual adjustment with the indicators – moving them up or down on the tippet to adjust the depth of the fly; clipping them smaller or larger to respond to "indicator-shy" behavior of the fish; and changing the color of the indicator to respond to the likelihood that a particular color is putting off a particular fish. In this latter category, my experience is that I can see the fluorescent green micro-indicator better than the red in most light conditions, but the fish appear to see it better as well. I often switch to a red indicator when I suspect that the green is off-putting, but rarely the other way around.

On the viewer's left (the right side of the vest), the traditional nippers resides, on its own retractor, between the dry fly spray and the fly tying scissors. The Gingher fly tying scissors are suspended at the "cap" of the scissors by a D-ring, while the actual scissors are on a retractor facing in the upward direction. On the viewer's right (the left side of the vest), the all-important diamond hone is on its own retractor (at the bottom right of the photo). Finally, the blue-handled pliers with smooth jaws (for bending barbs) is attached separately from the forceps with grooved jaws for pinching on the #8 split shot.

Other gear. Pay attention to the rest of your gear as well as the vest. For example, with the new breathable waders it is vitally important to have a pair of wicking polyester leggings (fly-weight) on your legs rather than a pair of cotton leggings. Never wear jeans under your waders (they will soak up and retain the sweat). Pull your socks on over the leggings so that the leggings won't bunch up as you pull on your waders.

Use studded wading shoes when fishing the spring creeks, if at all possible. But don't try to use the same wading shoes when you're floating the river in the guide's brand new drift boat – studded soles are NOT allowed on-board these crafts. If you're flying to Montana, then bring only the un-studded shoes. The studded shoes are a great device, however, to keep from slipping on the bowling ball, slime covered rocks of Armstrong's and DePuy's (they are probably less needed on Nelson's). But don't use slip-on rubbers with carbide studs or aluminum bars on your wading shoes – the silt will suck off these add-ons in nothing flat. And keep your wading shoes tied tightly and well – I've had to muck around in the muck to find one of my shoes when I've been too sloppy tying the laces.

Wading staffs should be considered, especially on the big, long pools of DePuy's. These long pools, such as the one below Betty's Riffle (or the pool above the rock dam on Nelson's), tend to deposit more silt than the shorter pools. Most anglers avoid wading in these pools, especially at the downstream end, because you can sink almost up to your knees in the silt. One friend almost died one day when he fell face down in the silt, with both wrists and both feet mired in the muck. I've fallen enough times so that now I always use a wading staff on DePuy's, one specially designed with a very wide diameter and a wide rubber tip, so that it doesn't sink very far down in the muck. This ungainly wading staff lets me fish sections of DePuy's that others don't fish, with the resulting satisfaction of getting over larger, less discerning fish. Suzanne solves the problem by using a belly boat in sections of DePuy's that others wade fish (such as the section immediately upstream of Dick's Pond). This sometimes gets the Trumpeter Swans excited – maybe they think that a competitor is after their forage – but the results are worth it. Indeed, belly-boating Dick's Pond itself is now standard procedure for several of the guides and you should try it if you have the chance.

On Armstrong's and Nelson's I now carry a thinner, fully-collapsible wading staff in a holster, which I use only as the day wears on and I find that I'm tiring and need the support of the wading staff when exiting the stream over the slime-covered rocks. Probably this summer, however, I'll transition to the wide-body wading staff on Nelson's as well as DePuy's – the rock-dam pool at Nelson's seems to be gaining more fish and no less silt as the years roll by, and I've become less certain of my ability to wade in the muck to go after the largest fish at the far margin of the creek.[41]

---

[41] Roger Nelson has done some wonderful stream improvement on the creek in recent years, creating wing dams that in turn have sped up the flow and reduced silt. Still, there is no way to remove the silt at the very downstream end of the pool at the rock-dam (short of breaking through the dam). At certain times of the day, there will always

Fly-boxes. The most important thing when preparing for a day on the spring creeks is to develop a "terminal tackle" plan. Which flies will I be imitating, which stages of these flies, and at what depth in the water column? The hatch charts for the creeks are well known and the hatch boards at the local fly shops are updated daily. So, no matter the day you choose, you'll have a very good idea of the major mayfly hatches and midge hatches, and you'll have your scud and sow-bug imitations ready for the "down" periods of the day. By the way, there are caddis hatches in Armstrong's and DePuy's, including the Mother's Day caddis hatch – although I've never seen enough of them to really get excited about them for more than a half-hour or so during the day. And, yes, during August, terrestrials can be useful, but I find that I never use them, when sight-fishing the scud produces as well as it does.

As we've discussed earlier, it almost doesn't matter where you enter the creek for the first time in the day. On Nelson's, upstream nymphing begins to get difficult earlier in the season than on the other two streams (perhaps because of the relatively greater area of flat water on this creek than on the others), but all this means is that, on Nelson's you'll be more likely to enter a section where you intend to cast a dry or a nymph in a <u>downstream</u> direction. Unless you plan on starting after the main mayfly hatch of the day, however, you'll almost certainly be starting during a period of few rises and you'll almost certainly be starting with one of the pheasant tail patterns. For this reason, I arrange my fly boxes in the following order: In the lower right hand pocket is the nymph and emerger box, with four foam leafs (counting the 2 sides of the swinging middle leaf of the box). One leaf holds weighted PT's, one leaf holds un-weighted but heavy wire hook PTs; one leaf holds un-weighted light-wire floating PTs, plus flush-floating emerger patterns; and the final leaf holds midge larvae, midge pupae, scuds and sow-bugs. In the next pocket of the vest are various true dry flies, but no spinners. This box has hinged-lid compartments, as in a Wheatley™ (although some Japanese boxes are now the near-equal of the English-maker's quality). The third box is all spinners. This box will have spinners of various sizes, body-color, and wing-type, as discussed in the chapter on imitations. The last box will be a hodge-podge of things, including the extremely small dries, such as the Troth mayfly emerger, the Troth midge emerger, some real "minority" flies (for the spring creeks) such as tricos, some small ants, etc. Sometimes a whole season will go by without me getting into this

---

be some frustratingly large fish on the far edges of that pool – fish that seem to take up a position guaranteed to sink you further into the silt as you try to reach them. I love it.

4th box – and I stopped carrying more than 4 boxes in my vest many years ago.

Your game plan for the day will be largely the same each day of the summer, but how you execute the plan will depend on what you see as you enter the creek, how the fish react to your choice of terminal tackle, and your application of the hypothetical "probability distribution" we discussed in Chapter 10 (on Midges). With that probability distribution in mind, your choice of which PT to start with will depend on what you see in the first 5 minutes after you've reached your first wading position. As your eyes adjust to the light conditions you'll concentrate first on how deep are the bulk of the fish – are there only a few rises but many elevated fish, or are there almost no rises and very few elevated fish. If it's the latter, then you'll probably start with a weighted pheasant tail.

As the pre-hatch period becomes more intense, the fish will certainly become more elevated and you'll certainly switch to a slightly sunken nymph tactic. And at the peak of the hatch, you'll be switching back and forth between the slightly sunken nymph, the floating nymph, the true emerger and the dun or crippled dun. And within each of these tactics you'll be making almost continual adjustments to the size and color of the micro-indicator and its distance from the fly. And when using the dry imitation – emerger, dun, or whatever – you'll be trying to have the fly reach the fish before the tippet. Once you've gained some experience, you'll be making these adjustments more frequently and quicker (that is, your mind will make the decision sooner to change your rig). Yet all of this is really simple when you boil it down to basics – you've got the right set of flies, you understand what is driving your choice of fly and tactic, and these choices, in turn, are driven by your ability to make the accurate cast with or without a reach cast. In other words you are adjusting your tactics on-the-go and doing so without having to waste long minutes appreciating what those trout are telling you. Again, your casting skills have let you reach the point of actually hearing what the trout are saying, and then, spending lots of days on the stream let you hear those words very clearly and very quickly. I often think of Datus Proper, and miss him, when my conversation with the trout is particularly informative.

15. American Heroes.

The Spring Creeks of Paradise Valley are known by enlightened anglers all over the world. While the creeks are almost other-worldly in their quality, they are not without controversy. Many anglers avoid the creeks not just because of the need to use highly technical fishing procedures, but also because of the per-day "rod" fees charged by the landowners. Some of these anglers are also staunch supporters of reasonable stream-access and, like me, support, in general, the Montana law that allows access, from public points such as bridges, to streams that otherwise flow through private property. The angler must either stay within the high-water mark when fishing a stream that flows through private property (assuming he has entered from a public place), or he must seek landowner permission to cross onto private land. For most of the major streams in Montana, this compromise seems workable, so long as the fisherman adheres to the rules and doesn't trash the banks of the stream he is fishing.

But some streams do not fit the mold and do not easily permit enforcement of the rules. The Beaverhead, for example, as a tail-water, maintains a fairly constant flow. It is nearly impossible for the wading or drifting angler (who wishes to stop to have lunch on the bank, for example) to avoid stepping onto private property. Private property rights have collided with anglers' desires more than once on this stream, on the Ruby, and on the Missouri below Holter Dam. However, I do not want to get into these issues in this book with regard to these other streams. I want to concentrate on Armstrong's, Nelson's, and DePuy's.

The spring creeks have a special quality that makes them essentially impossible for the "free" angler to fish them. There is no public access for the two stream-systems – Armstrong's-DePuy's (which is essentially the same creek), and Nelson's – except at their mouths where they flow into the Yellowstone River several miles south of Livingston. All of the remainders of the two systems – from their sources as springs (essentially holes in the ground), all the way to the Yellowstone, are on private land. Depuy's flows into the river on the West side of the Yellowstone, and Nelson's flows into the river on the East side. Further, Depuy's flows into the river through a simple culvert, since the volume of the creek is not all that large.[42]

Interestingly, Montana Fish, Wildlife, and Parks has been concerned that unfettered access to either stream would harm the reproduction of wild Yellowstone cutthroat trout. Apparently, some biologists believe that the two streams account for a very large percentage of the spawning grounds for the cutthroat that appear in a more-than-20 mile stretch of the Yellowstone, both upstream and downstream of the mouths of the creeks.[43] Worried that drifters on the Yellowstone would stop at the mouth of Nelson's, and walk up the center of the stream, the State has banned wading in the large gravelly section of the stream immediately above the mouth of Nelson's (and at other spots further upstream) during portions of the year prior to, during, and after the spawning season. This rule has gone a long way toward preserving the fragile eggs on the creek bottom, and also the landowners go to great lengths to make sure the people fishing upstream in their waters do not wade on these all-important gravel bars, except well after spawning.

Sometime in the early 1970's the Armstrong family (Agnes and Allen O'Hair) began to be concerned that the honor-system (in which non-paying anglers were supposed to limit their numbers to only 10 fishermen on the roughly ½ mile of creek) was not working. Sometimes the number of fishermen would be quite high and the angling experience suffered as a result. This led the family to start charging a small fee, initially $10, to keep the numbers of fishermen down, and to make sure they knew who was actually being permitted to cross their property, fish, eat lunch on the stream banks, pack out their trash, and use barless hooks while fly-

---

[42] Interestingly, all of the locals call the 3 streams by their owners' names – we would say "I fished Armstrong's today" or "Nelson's", or "DePuy's". Newcomers are apt to say things like "I fished the DePuy today", which sounds really strange over drinks. In writing about the streams, nevertheless, we often refer to their names as they appear in Fish and Game regulations -- Armstrong Spring Creek and Nelson Spring Creek. Since it does not appear in the annual regulations booklet, either DePuy's is not a stream under Montana regulations (because it is a completely artificial diversion of Armstrong water), or the State views it as part of Armstrong's.

[43] This view is not universally held. While it is clear that the spring creeks account for a large proportion of the spawning of the Yellowstone River's Rainbow population, some anglers believe that Cutthroat spawning is not important in the spring creeks. See, for example, Walinchus and Travis, p. 169. I don't have the slightest clue who is right about the importance of the creeks to cutthroat spawning (except to note that I see fewer cutthroats every year on the creeks), but their importance to rainbow and brown spawning is so evident that limited access makes sense to me.

fishing-only. Soon thereafter, or possibly earlier, the other two families started to emulate the Armstrong arrangement. By the mid-1970's the fame of the streams had spread, some would say, too far and too wide. To keep the number of people fishing to a manageable number, all three families started a formal reservation system and began to charge higher daily rod fees. In other words, the families began to duplicate the English system that had been in effect since the late 19th century to allocate scarce water on the Test and Itchen.

The English system may have served to keep the number of fishermen on the Test and Itchen to a seemly number, but there is also some possibility that the system had been aimed at a certain type of class-distinction system – essentially only wealthy Londoners and those of noble birth were invited to join the syndicates, at least in the early days. Not so with these American landowners. Any one from any walk of life can reserve a rod and pay the current fee. Over time, the families owning and managing the Livingston creeks learned that there were peak seasons to the hatches and therefore peak seasons to the demand for the scarce water. I like to think that I had something to do with this realization, since I spent so many years convincing Agnes O'Hair of the need to develop a peak-period pricing system. Now, at the start of the 21st century, you will pay a $100 per day rod fee (per fisherman or for fishermen that wish to literally share a single rod) during the peak period from June 15 through September 15. During the "winter period" – October 15 to April 15 – the rod fee is $40, and during the "phase-in" and "phase-out" periods (April 16 to June 14, then again from September 16 to October 14), the rod fee is approximately $75, depending on which particular stream you are fishing.

Also over the years, the reservation system of the 3 families has become well understood by the many guides and lovers of technical fly-fishing. You simply cannot get a rod reservation during the peak June 15 to middle of August period without reserving at least a year in advance, and some individuals act to reserve the same calendar days as they are leaving the creek for the last time each summer. This is very similar to the very best Alaska fly-out fishing lodges, except that $100 per day is a whole lot cheaper than the $1000 per day charged by the Alaska outfits. And Suzanne and I will continue to reserve at least a dozen days or so each year at this "exorbitant" rate, even if other business keeps us from enjoying the money we've spent (as during the financial crisis of 2007-2008 when I had to work many more hours than intended).

Still, many anglers think that the proletariat should rise up and make fee-fishing illegal. These anglers believe that it is there right to fish anywhere in the state, anytime for free. Maybe that is indeed a right on the many thousands of miles of large freestone streams that have blue-ribbon water in our state. But the Livingston spring creeks are very, very special and they are very, very scarce. The total available water on Nelson's and Armstrong's <u>combined</u> is only about one mile. DePuy's has something like 3 miles of water and the family allows 16 fishermen per day on this stretch. Nelson's allows 6 rods and Armstrong's 10 rods (plus up to another 10 rods or so for people that purchased some long-term fishing rights in the late 1960's and early 1970's attached to some home-sites across US 89). Thus, the number of fishermen per mile of these streams, during the height of the PMD and Sulphur hatches, exceeds those of most of the other major streams in the state. Still the fishing is extremely good, given the quality of the insect hatches, the fish-growing gravelly areas, and the constancy of the spring-water temperature.

What do you think would happen if anybody could fish these small, short streams for free? Wouldn't the stretches soon look like a New Jersey stocked trout stream on Opening Day? Is $40 or $100 too much to pay to guarantee that the angling experience is maintained, the quality of fishery preserved, the essence of "spring-creek fishing" allowed to seep into the minds and souls of those who give it a try? Shouldn't something this rare, this scarce, be allocated by a pricing mechanism, much as are golf courses, even municipal-owned links?

Now I know there are still many anglers in the state of Montana that would answer "NO" to these questions, even after reading these paragraphs. But I have some news for you -- you anglers that think a "free" thing is always a "good" thing. Each of the 3 families that run these reservation books on the Paradise spring creeks – each of the 3 – has received several offers over the years to sell the spring creeks to individuals or groups of individuals at prices in the many millions of dollars. The prices offered have been astounding – the wealthy groups would have to be paying, in foregone interest yield, more than something like $2,000 per day for each person to fish one of these creeks.[44] And why would these wealthy individuals or groups

---

[44] The math works out this way. Ted Turner buys several miles of Sixteen-Mile creek north of Bozeman. He may permit a couple of dozen friends to fish it, perhaps averaging 5 days each during the course of the year. Multiply those approximately 100 rod-days by ten, to be safe. Turner paid something in excess of $20 million for 16-mile, and I don't blame him. At 8% interest per year (the opportunity cost of investing that $20 million in the stock market over the decades), it costs him $1.6 million per year for the fishing – or something like that. This works out to over $1600 per rod per day. If you think Sixteen-Mile is worth that, how much is Nelson's worth, or

consider paying such an astounding amount? Because to them, the exclusivity of it, being able to be the ONLY people allowed to fish the creek in question, would be worth it.

And that's the crux of it. Neither the Nature Conservancy nor any other conservation group that would pay to own the spring creeks is willing to come anywhere near the true market value of these creeks, as demonstrated by actual offers that have been made. Moreover, the Nature Conservancy would likely run the purchased creek the way it runs Silver Creek -- any hundred or more fishermen can come fish on any day, for free. This angler-density is why fishermen say "if you think Armstrong fish are tough, try wading into the crowd at Silver Creek" Indeed, most professional guides on Silver don't take their clients to the actual creek – it's simply too crowded and difficult. So, they fish the spring lakes next to the creek out of belly boats. Not a "bad" thing, but not what most Armstrong Spring Creek or Nelson Spring Creek fishermen are thinking of when they buy their 2-weight rods.

Now ask yourselves, suppose you were the Nelsons, or the O'Hairs (Armstrong's), or the Smiths (DePuy's)? Why would you turn down that kind of money? Well, these folks are my friends, and I take what they say as the truth. When you cut right through it, there are two reasons. One, for sure, is that selling even a part of their ranches would cut at the soul of their lives – this ground and this water are what their ancestors named "Paradise" to begin with. But second, there is the acute realization that selling the creeks would effectively close them to the many thousands of anglers that cherish them, fish them, and are glad that the families do the hard work of running the reservation books and policing the trash and the occasional poor sport. The families are giving away hundreds of thousands of dollars of income each year to keep these streams open to the public.

If you don't believe that real altruism is at work here, try assuming that the creeks are filled to the maximum during each day of the main season, from June 15 through August 15, and that the creeks are 10% full the rest of the time. This is definitely NOT the case, since weather (as in 1996-1997), or the economy (as in 2008 and 2009) turn away hundreds of rod-days each

---

Armstrong's, or DePuy's? And, oh, by the way, you and I can't pay the $1600 to Ted to go fish there even if we wanted to. Maybe I would have done EXACTLY the same thing as Ted if I had his money. But the question is – why haven't the owners of the next stretch of Sixteen-Mile sold to him as well, or the owners of the 3 Livingston Spring Creeks? See the text above.

year. Meanwhile, 10 years of drought after the 1997 floods made the aquifer so low that weeds obliterated much of the creeks in August. Also, the arrogant rainbow trout serve to turn away quite a lot of other potential rods after their first time on the creeks – generally the people that don't go with guides, and even quite a few of those that do. The fact is that, except for the 2 month peak period, when 50-75% of peak capacity might be actually filled with real live fishing customers, the streams are generally close to empty. When you do the math, you realize that the annual revenue from the creeks would make no one wealthy.

When you compare this kind of revenue – maybe $50,000-$100,000 in a particularly great season for one of the streams with lots of luck -- against long-run stock market returns, the economics is all to advantage of the fisherman, not the owners. And even if you compare the revenues to earning only 3% in an insured savings account, the families are still losing quite a lot to continue to run their reservation books.

But, as any economist knows, revenues are not income. Expenses play a part as well. Now get this. During the aftermath of the 1996 flood, which affected primarily only the Armstrong system, the two families owning the Armstrong-DePuy system spent between $2 million and $3 million to repair the banks of the Yellowstone, in order to allow the spring creeks to function as separate waterways again. Concerned anglers who knew about the importance of the creeks' spawning areas, and knew that gaining a few more acres of river fishing was as nothing compared to losing the spring creeks that bring anglers from as far away as Japan and Russia, pitched in to form a tax-exempt fund into which donations were received from all over the world. But the total raised via these donations was very small compared with what the families had to spend.

And even during "normal" years, there is a continuous process of keeping siltation from claiming large expanses of fishable water. Each of the 3 families in the years since the floods has spent considerable time and money to reduce siltation and create new acres of rising fish. The O'Hair family reclaimed a large section of Armstrong's above the main spring; the Smiths reclaimed sections of DePuy's below the Blue Gate and in the Narrows (and are planning to create two braids of free-flowing stream around the periphery of what is now Dick's Pond, so that we fishermen will not have to risk our lives wading in the silt to reach those groups of rainbows feeding beyond our overly-long casts). At Nelson's, Roger has created several very deep pools that shelter the fish during the heat of August, with wing dams that speed up the current flow to remove silt. In each of these cases, a long permission-seeking process is necessary to obtain approvals from the State and Federal agencies involved. Heavy machinery is needed to move silt and earth. So far, I have not seen an instance in which the results of such work have interrupted the fishing in the affected areas for more than part of one season. And, after the waters calm down, the fishing has always been better than ever.

So, you see, it comes down to this. The families that own and manage these three world-class fisheries are nothing less than American Heroes. They have repeatedly turned down hard cash to do what's in all of our interests (although stories exist about a deal "coming close" in the past), and for this I will always be grateful. There will likely come a time, I think, when the economics of ranching and the economics of angling collide, and during some future generation, hopefully well down the line, the creeks will indeed be sold and closed to the public. It is my hope that there will be many more thousands of spring creek fly fishermen by then, people who may be able to help. But the reality of it is hard to ignore – in the decades to come, we fly fishermen should feel blessed to continue to have access to these rare gems. It will not last forever.

16. The Importance of Being … Upstream.

The summer of 2008 was a trying time – financially for the economy and for the fishing, because my work was taking up entirely too much of my time. Even though I'm blessed to be able to work out of the house, we fished only one day in August, one day in September, and the same in October. But the fish were talking their usual blue streak that summer and I learned some things in August and September that I had forgotten, or maybe never really learned.

On August 11, on Armstrong's, when I parked the car at the main parking lot, the big pool was empty save for one angler at the top of the riffle. So at roughly noon, I entered the middle of the pool and began working systematically up stream with upstream casts. There were almost no fish truly rising to the sparse remnants of the summer's PMD hatch, but I could see the usual large numbers of fish nymphing, some elevated and some not-so-elevated. They were all active, but feeding at a very leisurely pace. I chose to start with the several fish that were the most elevated, and so I tied on the usual olive PT, un-weighted, on a size 16. The Dai-Ichi large gape hook that Al had introduced us to really has a shank that is shorter for its gape than any other hook, so a size 16 fly really is more like a size 18 regular shank hook. I figured that there should be some active Baetis nymphs, prior to the mid-afternoon hatch of sulphurs. And the fish had already seen every nymph imitation in the world meant to duplicate the much larger PMDs. So the #16 short shank hook was a good compromise.

I had on 8x tippet, of course, plus a very small mini-micro-indicator. It was mid season and so my skill level was pretty high, it took me only a couple of casts to each fish to determine that I was being rejected – soundly. "OK", I reasoned, "we need to either go deeper or to another sub-surface fly. So I tied on a size 18 weighted olive PT, figuring that the deeper fish would be less selective and that the sulphur nymphs were at least a couple of hours away from starting their multiple trips to the surface. So fishing the nymph on the bottom made sense. But, same result. Not so much as a hesitation of the indicator. Moreover, a couple of times I could see the fish move out of the way of the micro indicator.

"Ah, it must be time to go indicator-less" I figured. So I picked out an elevated fish and made a perfect cast slightly to the left of a fish feeding no more than 15 feet up from me. When the fly should have been in the vicinity of the fish, it turned to its right, away from my fly. "Oh well, it must be that a natural caught its attention." So I made 3 more casts to within six inches of the same place, no more than a foot to the left of the fish and no more than 2 feet upstream of him. If he turned to the left I would set the hook even without an indicator or without seeing him open his mouth. Again, 3 times the fish turned to the right, not the left. Now, I knew I was not being deceived by light refraction, since I was casting straight upstream. Yes, the cast could have been wrong as far as distance, but not with respect to windage. Just to be sure, I made a couple of longer casts and couple of shorter ones. On the shorter casts the fish didn't move at all, and on the longer casts the fish moved again to its right.

I next figured that I must still be on the wrong fly, so in fairly rapid succession, after switching to another trout, I tried the slightly sunken midge pupa and the slightly sunken midge larva (although I saw no elevated larvae in the flow). I also did some indicator-fishing with the smallest micro-indicator that could be fashioned (I get better at fashioning these un-seeable indicators as the season progresses). I fished, with no more than 2 or 3 casts to each fish, over perhaps 30 fish for the next 90 minutes. It was past 1:30P.M. and I had not had a single hook-up, in the highest density pool on the creek, which I now had completely to myself! "My god, I thought, these fish sure have become more sophisticated than I ever thought possible – absolutely none of my tactics are working! I know the fish in this particular pool are among the toughest in the creek, since it is so accessible, clear, and slow. Is it possible I could get skunked in only the second week of August?" And then, the light bulb went on. Was it possible that these fish had become so tippet shy that even 8x, covering them before they saw the imitation, was enough to inform them of fakery?

So, somewhere around 1:30P.M. I turned around and faced downstream. There were still very few truly rising fish, very few bulging fish, but I could see several elevated, feeding fish below me, some of which I know I had failed to catch in my previous fishless minutes in the pool. I took off the midge pupa I was using, and put on an un-weighted olive PT, size 18, on the Tiemco 101 dry fly hook. I re-positioned the micro-mini-indicator to about 14 inches up from the fly. The first cast was to a visible rainbow about 20 feet down and to the right. I saw him open his mouth as the indicator came near to him. I lifted and a very nice fish shot out of the water and headed down to the bottom of the pool. It must have taken me 5 minutes to land that fish, then clean off the fly, squeeze some water out of the micro-indicator, put the landing net back in its place on my back, and get ready for the next target. A couple of more casts over another fish, this time on the left bank looking downstream, yielded the same result. For the next 3 hours I stayed in the big pool, working my way down to the very bottom, then re-starting at the riffle and working my way down to the place I had originally entered the pool. My total hook-ups were well north of 20 fish. Some were taken on a PT, some were taken on the midge pupa, some were taken on a floating nymph, and a couple trout were taken on the curved CDC emerger of Lee's. But every one was taken downstream. Every one was visibly seen before the cast (either as a bulging rise or a true rise or as the shape of a trout). Every one was a nice fish, and not every one made it into the net. A few were lost when the hook pulled out (I struck too soon or too late), and the 8x tippet broke twice, late in the day, when I had become tired and struck as if I were a novice.

That night, over dinner at the Chop House, I realized that I had indeed gotten an education. I had known for a long time that, at some point each summer – the specific time differing, depending on the creek or the specific pool or the kinds of "traffic" that had visited the pool -- downstream fishing was the only way to go. The fly must approach the fish before the tippet, all the while proceeding in a drag-free manner. Bob Berls and I had been discussing this just this past Spring via e-mail. Bob had gotten an e-mail from a friend on the West Branch of the Delaware in NY, saying that the very best fishermen were using 8x, fished downstream, to get their hookups. The "fish must see the fly before the tippet" one especially skilled angler had said, referring to either a nymph or dry fly on 8x.

And just a couple of weeks earlier than my August 11 trip to Armstrong's, in mid-July, Suzanne and I were fishing Nelson's with John Bailey. After a late lunch, I went up to fish the pools above the rock dam, and I could see that the midge hatch was going to be a good one. That afternoon I hooked up with plenty of fish, facing downstream, using the #18 red-ribbed black biot pupa. I could see John fishing downstream of me and he was also facing downstream, also hooking up frequently. Later, at the vehicles, as we were unstringing our rods, he said "boy, that was some of the finest midge pupa fishing I have ever had." So, here was one of the best dry fly men in Montana using not the Griffith's Gnat that I had assumed, but essentially the same fly as I was, both of us fishing the imitation slightly sunken, both of us facing downstream, both of us using the stop-cast to get perhaps, at most, a 2 foot drift. And both us were having a total blast.

So, what I learned the summer of the Great Recession is that the fish of the spring creeks are always learning just as we are. There are more and more skilled fishermen using extremely light tippets on well-tied flies. The fish can see or feel or sense the tiny splashes made by these tippets and flies, as the tippet lands across them or to the side of them – as it must if we are fishing upstream to the fish. No matter how careful the fisherman is – as I was on that August 11 – to not "line" the fish when casting upstream to him, the fish knows that something is wrong. In April, this knowledge certainly is not as finely honed in the small brain of the trout as it is in August. In April, upstream fishing with anything still works just fine – although, as the years go by, I seem to be detecting the need to start with 8x much earlier in the season than I had in the past. But no matter the size of the tippet, I have learned my lesson permanently now, regarding downstream fishing, and I shan't forget.

During the first week in September that year, I had my last day of the year on Armstrong's (generally, I fish during the winter months on a local's winter pass on DePuy's). Suzanne was recovering from gall bladder surgery and so chose to photograph, not fish. We arrived at the creek around noon, just as two guides, with their four fishermen were leaving the creek. I had Armstrong's all to myself that day, a gift that probably reflects how difficult the streams have become for the average fisherman. But it was a gift nevertheless, and one that I shall remember forever.

I started that day on what we call "my riffle," the one that begins the very long pool that ends with the riffle above the parking lot pool. I am quite sure that other fishermen call this riffle "my riffle," for it has not changed as much as other parts of the creek had in the floods of '96 and '97. It angles more away from the western bank of the creek than before, but it is always chock full of nice rainbows, except on this particular day. As I entered, I saw no feeders in the riffle. Perhaps they were stomped out by the 4 fishermen who had just left. So I tied on a size 18 PT on the obligatory 8x, and I started working my way downstream. In no more than a few minutes I began seeing lots of elevated small fish just below the riffle. I caught a dozen of these fish, all under 10", in no time flat, then I moved further down the pool, choosing to wade exactly down the center, because the light that day allowed me to see visible fish on either margin quite well.

Perhaps it was my wading down the middle, but that day there were very few visible fish exactly below me. Or perhaps there were many such fish but the light was wrong. But, that day, unlike any other I can remember on Armstrong's, I could see lots of nice fish, including some very nice rainbows, feeding VERY leisurely on sub-surface food in the shallow spots on either side of the pool. With an un-weighed PT on the Tiemco dry fly hook, I hooked up with almost every single one of those fish. Almost every one of the hooked fish had lots of fight in him, indicating that it had been a while since the fish had last been fooled. In 3 hours of fishing, my total was not huge, for these were all single fish, spotted, then stalked, in order to get the correct casting angle. Every single hook-up was to a fish for which the only chance was pure sight-fishing, watching the fish turn, or accelerate, to where I knew the fly to be. And there was usually at least 10 yards of empty shallow water along the bank until the next fish magically appeared. Each fish was cast to only once or twice, and each fish, when hooked, put up a hell of a fight. Because of their size, I felt obliged to follow several of them downstream and land them there. This was one reason why the total was not high, since the fighting always spooked a couple of other fish.

That day in September on Armstrong's, all alone, while Suzanne was photographing down the creek, on a bright, clear afternoon, with the mountains as my companions, turned into a day for the memory-bank. There have been other unforgettable days on this stream. One, more than thirty years ago was spent with my friend Dave Barry, a highly respected researcher on the trail of a cure for HIV. Dave went to college with me, was in our wedding party, spent years at the National Institutes of Health in Bethesda, and fished with us on the Pennsylvania lime-stoners and on the white fly hatch on the Potomac. That day on Armstrong's, there was a snow storm in September. There was also an unexpected egg-laying flight of caddis, and the four of us had the stream to ourselves, catching so many fish on top that it got downright ridiculous. Dave passed away recently, and Suzanne and I attended his funeral in Chapel Hill. At the ceremony, I told the story of that day on Armstrong's. Several hundred of Dave's colleagues in the audience probably didn't know what I was talking about. But I could see the faces of the fly fishermen in the crowd light up – Dave's brother, his uncle, and others. Today, I wonder about the other friends I've lost touch with; I wonder how many of them are still with us; how many of them might even fish the spring creeks occasionally without knowing that Suzanne and I are here, full time, hoping to make as many unforgettable trips to the stream as we are allotted.

172

References

1. Arbona, Fred L. Jr., <u>Mayflies, the Angler, and the Trout</u>, Lyons and Burford, NY, 1980, 1989.
2. Borger, Gary A., <u>Naturals</u>, Stackpole Books, Harrisburg, PA, 1980.
3. Brooks, Charles E., <u>Nymph Fishing for Larger Trout</u>, Crown Publishers, Inc. NY, 1976.
4. Best, A.K., <u>A.K.'s Fly Box</u>, Lyons and Burford, NY, 1996.
5. Caucci, Al and Bob Nastasi, <u>Hatches</u>, Comparahatch, Ltd., NY, 1973.·
6. Hafele, Rick and Dave Hughes, <u>The Complete Book of Western Hatches</u>, Frank Amato Publications, Portland, 1981.
7. Harrop, Rene, <u>Trout Hunter</u>, Pruett Publishing Company, Boulder, Colorado, 2003.
8. Juracek, John and Craig Matthews, <u>Fishing Yellowstone Hatches</u>, Blue Ribbon Flies, West Yellowstone MT, 1992.
9. Heck, Mike, <u>Spring Creek Strategies</u>, Headwater Books, New Cumberland, PA, 2008.
10. Lyons, Nick, <u>Spring Creek</u>, The Atlantic Monthly Press, NY, 1992.
11. Marinaro, Vincent C., <u>A Modern Dry Fly Code</u>, Crown Publishers, NY, fifth printing of 2nd edition, 1972, first edition published 1950.
12. Martin, Darrel, <u>Micropatterns</u>, Lyons and Burford, NY, 1994.
13. McCafferty, W. Patrick, <u>Aquatic Entomology</u>, Jones and Bartlett, Boston, 1983.
14. Osthoff, Rich, <u>Active Nymphing: Aggressive Strategies for Casting, Rigging, and Moving Nymphs</u>, Stackpole Books, Mechanicsburg, PA, 2006.
15. Pennak, Robert W., <u>Fresh Water Invertebrates of the United States</u>, Ronald Press Company, NY, 1953.
16. Proper, Datus, <u>What the Trout Said</u>, Alfred A. Knopf, NY, 1982.
17. Sawyer, Frank, <u>Nymphs and the Trout</u>, Crown Publishers, NY, second edition, 1970. (first edition published in 1958 by A. and C. Black Limited, London).
18. Shewey, John, <u>Mastering the Spring Creeks</u>, Frank Amato Publications, Portland, 1994.
19. Skues, G.E.M., <u>Nymph Fishing for Chalk Stream Trout and Minor Tactics of the Chalk Stream</u>, Adam and Charles Black, London, combined edition, 1970; first published in 1939 and 1910 respectively.
20. Swisher, Doug and Carl Richards, <u>Selective Trout</u>, Crown Publishers, NY, 1971.
21. Swisher, Doug and Carl Richards, <u>Emergers</u>, Lyons and Burford, NY, 1991.
22. <u>The Essential G.E.M. Skues</u>, edited by Kenneth Robson, Lyons Press, NY, 1998.
23. Walinchus, Rod and Tom Travis, <u>Fly Fishing the Yellowstone River</u>, Pruett Publishing Company, Boulder, Colorado, 1995.

Appendix: Contact information, if you are planning a trip to the Spring Creeks

Arranging a Guide. There are many fine guides in the Livingston-Bozeman area. My favorite guides are listed below. Lee Kinsey, Brant Oswald, and Tom Travis are the best of the best in my opinion. Tom, the oldest of the three, is legendary on the creeks. In his day, George Anderson was also a legend as a guide; he now owns and operates The Yellowstone Angler.

- Lee Kinsey: 406-220-3767 or 406-222-4494
- Brant Oswald: 406-222-8312
- Tom Travis: 406-222-2273
- Al Gadoury: 406-586-3806
- John Greene: 406-222-3562

Other great guides are out there and any omission is not intentional -- I simply do not know their names or have not seen them actually working on the creeks. Still other good guides I know have retired from what is a very tough profession. So please contact the local fly shops about availability and be specific about wanting a guide with substantial spring creek experience.

Not only can you hire guides at the fly shops in Livingston, you should also buy some of your flies there, especially if you don't fish spring creeks in your home State. I list only the Livingston and Yellowstone Valley fly shops, but there are great shops in Bozeman too, so stop in to those on your way over from the airport. Of these fly shops, the best fly collection is found at Buzz Basini's Spring Creek Specialists on DePuy's. Turn off Highway 89 on the O'Hair access road as if heading to Armstrong's, then take the first left and go down to the creek. But round out your collection at the other local shops as well.

Fly shops in Livingston and down the Valley.

- Spring Creek Specialists: 406-222-5664 or www.springcreekspecialists.com
- George Anderson's Yellowstone Angler: 406-222-7130 or www.yellowstoneangler.com
- Dan Bailey's (a must if you are in town for any reason): 406-222-1673 or www.dan-bailey.com
- Sweetwater Fly Shop: 877-628-FISH or www.sweetwaterflyshop.com
- Hatch Finders Fly Shop: 406-222-0989 or www.hatchfinders.com
- Angler's West (Emigrant): 406-333-4401 or www.montanaflyfishers.com
- Park's Fly Shop (Gardiner): 406-848-7314 or www.parksflyshop.com

- Yellowstone Gateway Sports (Livingston and 4-Corners): 406-222-5414

Again, my apologies for any omissions; none were intentional. Besides, there is no such thing as a fly shop not worth visiting.

Spring Creek Reservations.

You can obtain reservations with the guides, through the fly shops, or calling the stream managers directly. Here are the stream telephone numbers. The earlier in the year you reserve, the better are your chances of getting a date during the peak of the season from June 15 through August or so. It is always better to reserve a date a year in advance if possible.

- Armstrong Spring Creek: 406-222-2979
- Depuy's Spring Creek: 406-222-0221 or www.depuyspringcreek.com
- Nelson's Spring Creek: 406-222-6560 or www.nelsonsspringcreek.com

Also, some of the fly fishing lodges in the area book their own days on the streams specifically for their guests, and they provide guides as well. Several lodges operate in the Valley and you can have your pick as to size, location, price, etc. Two that have been highly recommended to me by my own guests are:

- Hubbard's Yellowstone Lodge 406-848-7755
- Mountain Sky Guest Ranch 406-333-4911

There are dozens of other, smaller lodges and B&B's that you can Google, some with guide connections and shuttle services so you can combine a trip to the spring creeks with a float on the Blue Ribbon portion of the Yellowstone, or a day or two in Yellowstone National Park. If you do stay at one of the lodges, however, be very careful about the spring creek experience of your guide. If the guide does not have several years of experience on the creeks, don't be afraid to sign up one of the more experienced guides not affiliated with the lodge (the lodge will not pick up this guide fee, in most instances). Note also that the fishing is quite varied in Park County and adjoining areas, and includes several very nice spring lakes, some of which can be reserved through the fly shops.

Enjoy good fishing, and look me up if you see a Suburban with either of the following license plates at one of the spring creeks -- 8X or BAETIS.

Acknowledgments

I've tried to learn something from everybody I've ever fished with, not just Al Troth. People like John Fiorini, Frank Smith and dozens of folks at the Washington, DC chapter of Trout Unlimited helped me in my formative years, after Bob Wallace and John Wicks in Missoula got me started on the western streams. Indeed, it was a fellow grad student back East -- Barry Rogstad -- who taught me how to use my fly rod to cast real flies, not a baited hook, some 44 years ago.

Others here in Montana added to my knowledge, including especially Pete Cardinal, the Dean of the Missouri below Holter. My patient wife and partner, Suzanne, should be credited with many of the techniques in this book, because our discussions during and after each day of fishing led both of us to continually improve. A long line of guides in many places, such as Lindsay White in New Zealand, taught me about finding fish and deciding on a tactic for each one. In the last decade or so, discussions with Lee Kinsey, Brant Oswald, Buzz Basini, and many others, helped to refine techniques. Watching Mike Copeland, John Bailey, Al Gadoury, John Greene or Tom Travis actually fish the spring creeks helped immensely. I watched George Anderson teach a 12-year boy to fly-cast once in the parking lot at Armstrong's, and he had the kid catching trout later the same morning. Gary Borger showed us how to work a leech pattern in Armstrong's one day. I learned things from teaching our own boys, John David and Daniel, how to fish the spring creeks, and at one point in his young life Daniel thought he was better than his old man. And then there were other anglers that helped as well, simply by doing things which did NOT work and which re-enforced what I already knew.

But it was Bob Berls who taught me almost as much as Al, by continually informing me of new literature, introducing us to strike indicators, arranging trips to the English chalk streams and their informed devotees such as Ian Mackintosh of the upper Itchen. It was Bob who made it clear what Skues and Sawyer had started so very long ago. It was Bob who nagged me about finally writing this book, who edited it more than once, and corrected misspellings and sloppy construction. Bob Berls is probably the most well-read fly angler in the States, and he can hold his own, and does, with anglers at the Flyfishers' Club of London, on the salmon rivers of Russia, and on the clear waters of the South Island.

About the Author and His Colleagues

John Mingo. John has spent over 40 years fly-fishing in more than 30 of the states, including Alaska and most of the states with great spring creeks or tail waters. He has fly-fished for trout in England, Austria, New Zealand, Patagonia, and Tierra del Fuego, and for bonefish in the Bahamas and the Yucatan. He has spent over 1000 days on the Montana spring creeks and written several articles for *Fly Fisherman* magazine on the subject.

John's day job is as an expert on the regulation of risk in banking. He has been a Senior Advisor to the Federal Reserve Board, and a Deputy Assistant Secretary of the Treasury. He holds a B.A. in economics from Yale, and a Ph.D., also in economics, from Brown.

Suzanne Mingo. Suzanne holds a B.A. in history from Albertus Magnus College and an M.A. in education from Bridgeport University. She has taken graduate level courses in photography, and has taught photography to middle-school students in Bethesda, Maryland. Over the last 25 years she has pursued her specialty of large-format fine-art photography. While the photos in Rainbows of Paradise were taken mostly with 35mm Nikon digital equipment, she spends most of her time with medium format Hasselblads and large format Linhof cameras. Her darkroom contains equipment by Beseler and LPL, and enlarging lenses by Schneider.

Suzanne is an expert in the Ansel Adams Zone System and has studied with John Sexton at his annual workshop in Snowmass at the Anderson Ranch, and at his studio in Carmel. She has had several shows at the well-regarded Danforth Gallery in Livingston. Her photos have appeared in *The Washington Post*, *Fly Fisherman* magazine, *The Bulletin* of the Angler's Club of New York, and The National Parks Fishing Guide by Robert Gartner. You can see more of her work at www.RainbowsPhotography.com.

Lee Kinsey. Lee is a 4th generation Montanan, raised in Big Timber, who essential grew up by fly-fishing the Yellowstone and the Boulder. He attended college at the Montana School of Mines, and, fortunately for us, did not take up mining after an internship in Colorado fell through. He learned to tie wonderful flies under the tutelage of Paul Redfern, owner of the Fish On! shop in Butte. Early on, Lee was fortunate enough to have Al Troth inspect his flies and offer suggestions. A small shadowbox of Al's flies were loaned to Lee by Paul, and he practiced until his own flies looked just like Al's.

Lee took up guiding after his mining career stopped short, and has been at it ever since -- some 14 years in total. His first efforts at guiding on the spring creeks were a "trial by fire" as he puts it. As he went along, he found that most of the flies used on the spring creeks were "archaic" in his words. Some 700+ spring-creek-days later, he now finds that, on his days off, he is more interested in trying new flies on the creeks rather than catching trout on what he knows will work.

Lee lives in Livingston with his wife Abby and daughter Libby. He often thanks Paul Redfern for teaching him how to tie and for introducing him to Paul's niece, who later became Lee's wife. Lee owns the outfitting service Secluded Water and has some of the finest private-access water in this part of the country. If you want to get on his list for custom flies or these waters, do it soon. He can be reached at 406-220-3767, or via lee@wispwest.net.

Mark Susinno. Mark holds a Bachelor of Fine Arts in painting from Pratt Institute. Working as a fabricator of bullet-proof doors in 1985, he entered and won the Maryland Trout Stamp contest and decided to pursue his art full time. Since then his work in oils and acrylics, coupled with his expertise in fly-fishing, has led him to many honors, including designing 22 state fishing stamps and covers/illustrations in all the major fishing journals, including *Gray's Sporting Journal, Sporting Classics, Field & Stream, Sports Afield, Fly Fisherman*, and many others. His works have graced Lefty Kreh's Advanced Fly Fishing Techniques and Ultimate Guide to Fly Fishing, and Alan Robinson's Ode to Bass & Trout. Since 1987, Mark's limited edition prints have been published by Wild Wings, LLC.

Mark's fly-fishing interests have led him to Alaska, Labrador, Scotland, and many other North American sites, including to coastal waters for tarpon, bonefish, snook, stripers, blues, and dolphins. He especially loves to fish for smallmouth near his home in Harrisburg, Pennsylvania. Mark is a member of the Society of Animal Artists and American Mensa. The interested reader can see more of his work, including the original oil painting used for this book's cover art, by visiting www.natureartists.com/susinnom.htm.

Robert Berls. Bob holds degrees from Wesleyan and Yale Universities and is retired from Federal service in Washington, D.C. He has fished for trout in 13 states, including Alaska, and in England and New Zealand. Bob has fished for the huge sea-run brown trout in Tierra del Fuego and for Atlantic salmon in Canada and Russia. He has bonefished in Belize, Florida, and the Bahamas. Bob is the long-time editor of the *Bulletin* of The Anglers' Club of New York and writes the "Letter from America" for the *Flyfishers' Journal* of the Flyfishers' Club of London.